Henry Home Kames

Loose Hints Upon Education

Chiefly concerning the culture of the heart. Second Edition

Henry Home Kames

Loose Hints Upon Education
Chiefly concerning the culture of the heart. Second Edition

ISBN/EAN: 9783337424169

Printed in Europe, USA, Canada, Australia, Japan

Cover: Foto ©Suzi / pixelio.de

More available books at **www.hansebooks.com**

LOOSE HINTS

UPON

EDUCATION,

CHIEFLY CONCERNING THE

CULTURE

OF THE

HEART.

SECOND EDITION,
ENLARGED.

Train up a Child in the way he should go; and, when he is old, he will not depart from it.   PROV. xxii. 6.

EDINBURGH:

PRINTED FOR JOHN BELL, PARLIAMENT-SQUARE;
GEO. ROBINSON, PATERNOSTER-ROW,
AND JOHN MURRAY, LONDON.

M,DCC,LXXXII.

TO THE

QUEEN.

DURING childhood, every object strikes the mind with the force of novelty; and the mind, soft like wax, yields to every impression, good or bad. To cherish the former and to prevent the latter, is the province of the mother; for as she is entrusted by Providence with the government of her children during their tender years,

the

the mind ought to be no lefs her care than the body.

The children of Princes are in a critical ftate with refpect to education: they have none but their mother to preferve them from the corruption of flattery and fawning. If they have loft her early, they are undone.

It has fallen to your Majesty's lot, to take the lead in the education of a numerous and hopeful Royal Family; and if fame fpeak true, Providence has not in referve a perfon more worthy of that important office: it is laborious indeed, but pleafing to a mother.

May

May Heaven, profpering your maternal tendernefs and perfeverance, make your children what you wifh them to be, affectionate to their parents, kindly to their dependents, and in time illuftrious examples of good conduct to the Britifh nation.

A Royal Family fo educated may be relied on as a firm fupport to the Throne.

THE purpofe of this Effay is to evince, that the culture of the heart during childhood, is the chief branch of education. I have little doubt of convincing thofe who are difpofed to give attention; but dry fubjects feem at prefent not to be in requeft.

requeſt. One ſure way there is to procure attention; and I know no other. If your MAJESTY will gracciouſly condeſcend to patroniſe this little Work, it will become faſhionable: every one will read: a number will approve; and perhaps a few will ſeriouſly think of a reformation.

BUT imitation is more perſuaſive than exhortation. Though in this degenerate age, our women of faſhion, neglecting domeſtic concerns, ſeem to think every hour loſt that does not paſs in a crowd; yet your MAJESTY's exemplary conduct cannot fail to have great influence. Many it will reclaim to a more ſedate

date and more rational tenor of life; and your proselytes, happy in the change, will chearfully testify to the world a sacred truth, That a mother's sweetest pleasure, arises from preparing her children, by virtuous education, to be happy in this life, as well as in the life to come.

May your Majesty's life be long and prosperous, not only for your own sake, but for that of our Sovereign, of your Royal Issue, and of the Nation.

Your devoted Subject,

Henry Home.

CONTENTS.

                                                              Page.

Introduction - - - 1

Episode upon the Duty of Women to nurse their own Children - - 30

SECT. I.

Authority of Parents - - 47

SECT. II.

Management of Children in the First Stage of Life - - 58

SECT. III.

Management of Children in their Second Stage - - - 75

SECT. IV.

Management of Children in their Third Stage - - - 102

SECT. V.

Instructions that occasionally may be applied in every Stage - - 141

SECT. VI.

Peculiarities respecting the Education of Females - - - 160
Appendix to Section VI. - - 168

SECT. VII.

Education with respect to Religion 188
Appendix to Section VII. - - 208

SECT. VIII.

Instructions preparatory to the married State - - - - 249

SECT. IX.

Instructions concerning the Culture of the Head or Understanding - 260

SECT. X.

Short Essays on particular Subjects relative to the Culture of the Heart 281

CONTENTS.

ARTICLE I. *Selfishness and Benevolence compared* - - - 281

ARTICLE II. *Opinion and Belief less influenced by Reason than by Temper and Education* - - 289

ARTICLE III. *Differences in Opinion make the Cement of Society* - 301

ARTICLE IV. *Partiality* - - 313

ARTICLE V. *Association of Ideas* - 327

APPENDIX I.

Things to be got by Heart for improving the Memory - - - 339

APPENDIX II.

Excerpts from a young Gentleman's Common-place-book; being the History of his First Excursion after completing his College Education - - 387

LOOSE HINTS

ON

EDUCATION,

CHIEFLY CONCERNING THE

CULTURE OF THE HEART*.

INTRODUCTION.

THE mind of man is a rich soil, productive equally of lovely flowers and noisome weeds. Good passions and impressions are flowers which ought carefully to be cultivated: bad passions and impressions

---

* The Head is the seat of thinking, deliberating, reasoning, willing, and of all other internal actions. The Heart is the seat of emotions and passions; and of moral perceptions, such as right and wrong, good and bad, praise and blame, &c. See Elements of Criticism, edit. 5. vol. II. page 507.

impreffions are weeds which ought to be difcouraged at leaft, if they cannot be totally rooted out. Such moral culture is no flight art: it requires a complete knowledge of the human heart, of all its mazes, and of all its biaffes.

As impreffions made in childhood are the deepeft and the moft permanent, the plan of our Creator for giving accefs to the heart, even in that early period, cannot be too much admired. The firft thing obfervable is, an innate fenfe that enables us to difcover internal paffions from their external figns*. As that fenfe is of prime ufe in every period of life, it is early difplayed; indeed as early as the fenfes of feeing and hearing. An infant on the breaft difcerns good or bad humour in its nurfe, from their external figns on her countenance, and from the different tones of her voice. Next, thefe figns

---

* Elements of Criticifm, edit. 5. vol. I. p. 441.

signs and tones affect the infant differently: a song or a smile, chears it: a harsh look or tone, makes it afraid, or keeps it in awe.

By these means, the human heart lies open to early instruction; and is susceptible of having proper notions stamped on it, such as those of right and wrong, of praise and blame, of benevolence and selfishness, of yours and mine. The great utility of such notions, will appear from opposing them to various absurd notions and opinions, which never could have prevailed in the world, had they not been inculcated during infancy. Take the following instances. Stories of ghosts and hobgoblins heard for the first time by one grown up, make no impression unless it be of laughter; but stamped on the mind of a child, they harass it incessantly, and are never wholly obliterated. Many Popish doctrines are contradictory to common sense; and yet held to be self-evident, because they were instilled during childhood. What is it that can rivet in the mind of any one the strange doctrine of transubstantiation, but the taking advantage of early youth, which is susceptible equally of every impression, right or wrong? Were that doctrine reserved for adult persons, it would be rejected by all for its eminent absurdity. The low people in Spain have little other notion of a Christian, but of one who signs himself with the cross; and yet are prone to blood and slaughter against every person who forbears that trifling ceremony. When notions that have no foundation in nature take such hold of the mind, it cannot be doubted but that notions grafted on some natural principle or affection will be equally permanent. Therefore, let it be the first care of parents, to instil into their children right notions, which can be done by looks and gestures,

gestures, even before a child is capable of understanding what is said to it. With regard to families of distinction in particular, this branch of education is of the highest importance. Even before the age of seven, notions of rank, of opulence, of superiority in the children of such families, begin to break out, and to render them less obsequious to discipline than in their more tender years: if admitted to take peaceable possession, adieu to education of any sort.

ROUSSEAU advances a strange opinion, that children are incapable of instruction before the age of twelve. This opinion, confined to the understanding, is perhaps not far from truth. But was it his opinion, that children before twelve are incapable of being instructed in matters of right and wrong, of love and hatred, or of other feelings that have an original seat in the heart? If it was, gross must have

have been his ignorance of human nature. And yet that this was really his opinion, appears from his infisting that a child ought not to be punished for telling a lie; which can have no foundation, other than that a child is not confcious of doing wrong when it tells a lie, more than when it tells truth. If the moral difference between truth and falfehood be innate, which it furely is, why ought not a child to be punished for telling a lie, if the vice cannot be reftrained by gentler means?

INFANCY is a bufy fcene, and yet little attended to, except for the fake of health. As this period is fhort, every opportunity ought to be taken, for inftilling right notions and making proper impreffions. The infant, at the fame time, is bufy in gathering for itfelf a ftock of ideas from the various objects of the external fenfes, ready to be uttered as foon as it can fpeak, which it can do commonly before the age of two: the difficulty it has to ſtruggle with, is not want of ideas, but want of words. It is wonderful to what degree of underſtanding ſome children arrive very early. A child named Martha, three years old, had been told jocularly, that Martha or Mattie was an ugly name, and that ſhe ought to have been called Matilda. The child was overheard ſaying to a younger ſiſter, who had not yet got the uſe of her tongue, " When you can ſpeak, " you muſt not call me Mattie, but Ma- " tilda." There are inſtances without number of the ſame kind; and in tracing the progreſs of the mind, they deſerve well to be recorded.

THE education of girls is by nature entruſted to the mother; and of boys, till they are fit for regular diſcipline at ſchool. The father occaſionally may give a helping hand, but it can only be occaſionally.

THUS

INTRODUCTION.

Thus the culture of the heart during childhood, the moſt precious time for ſuch culture, is a taſk with which females only are charged by Providence; a vocation that ought to employ their utmoſt ſagacity and perſeverance; a vocation not inferior in dignity, as will appear afterward, to any that belongs to the other ſex. Yet children, during that precious time, are commonly abandoned to nurſes and ſervants. The mother is indeed attentive to the health of her child; and flatters herſelf that nothing further is required from her. But it cannot be expected, that early education will be regarded by a mother who is ignorant of its advantages.

This is deplorable, eſpecially as there are ſeveral obſtacles to a remedy. One is, that there is no ſchool, public or private, for teaching the art of cultivating the heart. Nor is it an art of a ſlight kind:

INTRODUCTION.

kind: few arts are more complicated or more profound. Another is, that this art, as the world goes, appears to be little in requeſt; and, I believe, is ſeldom thought of in chuſing a wife. A young man, inclined to avarice, diſcovers no virtue in a young woman but a plentiful fortune. Another, addicted to the pleaſures of ſenſe, regards beauty only. A prudent man, having nothing in view but an agreeable companion, is ſatisfied with a ſweet temper and affable manners. The art of training up children is never thought of, though of all the moſt eſſential in a mother.

ZEAL to have ſuch obſtacles removed, ſuggeſted to me the following Eſſay. Senſible I am, that in its preſent looſe attire, it is ſcarce fit to appear in public; but may not the uncertainty of life in an advanced age, plead my excuſe? I ſhould have died with regret, had any thing been

been left undone by me, that could benefit my fellow creatures. Were it generally understood, that the education of children is the mother's peculiar province, an important trust committed to her by her Maker, education during that early period, would, I am persuaded, be carried on more carefully than it is at present. With respect to the education of female children in particular, genteel accomplishments, such as music and dancing, need not be rejected; but in order to accomplish them as mothers, the knowledge of human nature and the art of improving the heart, ought chiefly to be insisted on. This art would have a beneficial influence on the conduct of married women. Instead of roaming abroad for want of occupation at home, the dignified occupation of educating their children, would be their most charming amusement. The husband, happy in his wife and in his children, would in no other place find the

comfort

comfort of his own houfe. The children, early infpired with morality and religion, would be prepared to perform with alacrity every duty, and to ftand firm againft every temptation.

How diftant from fuch a ftate are perfons in high life, who, in great cities, are engaged in a perpetual round of pleafure! Take for inftance routs and card-affemblies. Excepting thofe at the card-tables, who make but a fmall part of the company, the reft faunter about, looking at one another, wifhing in vain to have fomething to fay. Whether frequency does not render fuch meetings wofully infipid, I appeal to thofe who pafs much of their time in them. And yet, for fuch paftime, married women not only neglect domeftic œconomy, but even the education of their children.— Unhappy mortals to be thus deluded by a mere fhadow! Their only refource for their children,

dren, is a boarding school; which is not a little hazardous for girls, who by their number escape strict attention; and who, in the most ticklish period of life, are more apt to follow bad example than good. Young ladies of rank, carried from the boarding school to the dissipation of high life, are not likely to behave better than their mothers did before them. The fruits of such education are but too apparent. Formerly, neither divorce nor separation were much heard of: they have now become so frequent, as scarce to make a figure in a news-paper. A young woman engaged in affection to a lover, is forced by her parents into what is termed a more advantageous match. Nature prevailing over conscience, she yields to her lover against her duty. That miserable woman is surely entitled to some share of pity; but a lady who lives always in public, seldom has that excuse for deserting her husband. Genuine love is a tender plant that cannot even take root in a crowd; for an impreſſion, if made, is baniſhed by the next new face. Young women in high life are married at the will of their parents, without any perſonal attachment; and if one of them go aſtray, ſhe has not love for an excuſe, but downright appetite for variety. It is not difficult, I ſuſpect, to find ſuch a woman, who would prefer her huſband before her gallant, were they equally new to her. Oh! Babylon, Babylon, the terror of nations, but the ſink of iniquity.

Bidding adieu to ſuch perſons as irreclaimable, I cannot deſpair of a reformation in the more ſober part of the female ſex, if the importance of cultivating the heart of their children be ſet in a clear view. My expectations are the more ſanguine, from my acquaintance with ſeveral women of diſtinction, who conſider the

the education of their children as their indispensable duty, and who take great delight in it. One lady there is of high rank, whom I forbear to name, being afraid of displeasing her. I should otherways propose her as a pattern, not merely for imitation, but for emulation: to excel her, instead of pain, would give her satisfaction. I cannot readily form a wish more beneficial to my fellow citizens, than that her talent for educating children should become general; and be exercised by every mother with that lady's skill and perseverance.

It appears unaccountable, that our teachers generally have directed their instructions to the head, with very little attention to the heart. From Aristotle down to Locke, books without number have been composed for cultivating and improving the understanding: few in proportion

INTRODUCTION.   15

proportion for cultivating and improving the affections. Yet surely, as man is intended to be more an active than a contemplative being, the educating of a young man to behave properly in society, is of still greater importance than the making him even a Solomon for knowledge. Locke has broached the subject, and Rousseau has furnished many ingenious hints. The following Loose Thoughts on the same subject, are what have occurred to me occasionally.

GOOD education may be illustrated by comparing it with its opposite. The following account is given by Le Brun of those kings of Persia who have inherited by blood. " This king is absolute
" in the strictest sense; for he disposes
" of the lives and properties of his sub-
" jects without control. He is born in
" the seraglio, and kept there in prison,
" ignorant of what passes in the world.
                              " When

"When arrived at a certain age, he is
"taught to read and write by a black
"eunuch, is inftructed in the Maho-
"metan faith, and to bear an impla-
"cable hatred to the Mahometans of
"Turkey and of Indoftan; but not a
"fyllable of hiftory, of politics, nor even
"of morality. Far from being teafed
"with things that require application,
"he is fet loofe to fenfual pleafure the
"moment the impulfe takes him. Opium
"is procured for him, and other drugs
"that excite voluptuoufnefs. At the
"death of his predeceffor, he is led
"from his prifon to the throne, where
"all proftrate themfelves before him,
"with expreffions of the moft abject fer-
"vility. Surprifed, nay ftupified, with
"a fcene fo new and extraordinary, he
"conceives all to be a dream; and it re-
"quires time to render the fcene fami-
"liar. As he is incapable of infpiring
"affection or even good will, his cour-
"tiers

"tiers have no view but to make a pro-
"perty of him. Far from offering him
"good advice, they keep him ignorant
"in order to mislead him. Thus the Per-
"sian kings pass their vigour in luxury
"and voluptuousness, without the least
"regard to their people or to their own
"reputation." Carneades the philosopher observed, "that the sons of princes
"learn nothing to purpose but to ride
"the great horse; that in other exercises
"every one bends to them; but that a
"horse will throw the son of a king with
"no more remorse than of a cobler."
Must I be obliged to think, that the foregoing description, with a few slight va-
riations, may suit the greatest part of
those who, in France and England, were
born with the certainty of inheriting a
great estate? "If there is any characte-
"ristic peculiar to the young people of
"fashion of the present age, it is their
"laziness, or an extreme unwillingness
"to

" to attend to any thing that can give
" them trouble or difquietude; with-
" out any degree of which they would
" fain enjoy all the luxuries of life, in
" contradiction to the difpofitions of
" Providence, and the nature of things.
" They would have great eftates without
" any management, great expences with-
" out any accounts, and great families
" without any difcipline or œconomy:
" in fhort, they are fit only to be inhabi-
" tants of *Lubberland*, where, as the child's
" geography informs us, men lie upon
" their backs with their mouths open, and
" it rains fat pigs, ready roafted." *The
World*, No. 157. Lord Chefterfield, the
moft agreeable of writers, expreffes himfelf with peculiar fpirit upon a different
branch of this character. "As for the mo-
" dern fpecies of human bucks, I impute
" their brutality to the negligence or to
" the fondnefs of their parents. It is
" obferved in parks among their betters,
" the

INTRODUCTION. 19

"the real bucks, that the most trouble-
"some and mischievous are those who
"were bred up tame, fondled, and fed
"out of the hand, when fawns. They
"abuse, when grown up, the indulgence
"they met with in their youth; and
"their familiarity grows troublesome and
"dangerous with their horns *."

FEW

---

* A young man born with the certainty of succeeding to an opulent fortune, is commonly too much indulged during infancy, for submitting to the authority of a governor. Prone to pleasure, he cannot bend to the fatigues of study: his mind is filled with nothing but plans of imagined happiness, when he shall have the command of that great fortune. No sooner is he in possession, than he sets loose all his appetites in pursuit of pleasure. After a few years of gratification, his enjoyments by familiarity and easiness of attainment become languid, and at length perfectly insipid. In the mean time, a total neglect of œconomy reduces him to straits, his debts multiply and become urgent; and he is in the highest flow of dissipation, when his enjoyments are at the lowest ebb. Dissimulation now supplants the native candour of his temper. He must promise when he knows he cannot perform, and must caress a dun who is his aversion. Despairing to retrieve his affairs, he abandons himself to profligacy: his peace of mind is gone; and

he

INTRODUCTION.

Few articles concerning government are of greater importance, than good education.

he is now more wretched than formerly happy. Oppose to this meteor, a young man without fortune, who must labour for his bread. He is educated to a calling which he prosecutes with industry, but for some time with little profit. By perseverance his circumstances becoming easy, he thinks of marriage. He delights in his wife and children; and his grand object is to make a fortune for each of them. They are all put into a good way of living. One of his sons is assumed as his partner in business; upon whom by degrees is devolved the laborious part. And now, our merchant finds ample leisure to indulge in the comforts of society. He ends his days with a grateful sense of the goodness of Providence, in bestowing blessings on him with a liberal hand. Let us compare.—But there is no comparison. No man of sense would chuse to be the person first described. A man on the contrary must be ambitious beyond measure, who would not be satisfied with the lot of the other. I can figure no state more happy, if it be not that of a man who for years has applied himself to business, sweetened by a taste for letters. Fortune throws into his lap a large estate, of which he had no expectation. Having been taught by experience that his own wants are easily supplied, he exerts his usual industry to make his friends happy, and to remedy the wants and distresses of his fellow creatures. Can any state be figured more opposite than this to that first mentioned, with respect to every comfort of life?

cation. Our moral duties are circumfcribed within precife bounds; and therefore, may be objects of law. But manners, depending on an endlefs variety of circumftances, are too complex for law; and yet upon manners chiefly depends the well-being of fociety. This matter was well underftood among the ancient Romans. Out of the moft refpectable citizens were elected cenfors, whofe province it was to watch over the manners of the people, to diftinguifh the deferving by fuitable rewards, and to brand with difgrace every grofs tranfgreffion. But in an opulent nation, it is vain to think of ftemming the tide of corruption. To give vigour to the cenforian office, it indifpenfably muft be exercifed by men of dignity, eminent for patriotifm, and of a character above exception. But as fuch men were not to be found among the degenerate Romans, the office vanifhed, and has not been revived in any modern

dern government: nor, indeed, does there exift any government fo pure, as to admit that delicate inftitution. Our only refource for exercifing that important office, are fathers and mothers. May it fink into their hearts, that we have no reliance but upon them for preventing univerfal corruption, and of courfe diffolution of the ftate. It might indeed have been expected, that the parental cenforian office fhould be countenanced and encouraged by people in power. Though the legiflature can do little, the Sovereign and his minifters may do much, both by example and precept. It is in their power to bring domeftic difcipline into reputation, which would excite parents to redouble their diligence. Much need, alas! is there for fome fuch exertion, confidering the defective ftate of education in this ifland. So little notion have the generality of its importance, that if a young heir get but a fmattering of Latin or of French, he is held

held to be an accomplished gentleman, qualified for making a figure. What if a person who hath carefully bred up a family, and added to the society a number of virtuous citizens, male and female, should be distinguished by some mark of honour, which, at the same time, would add lustre to every individual of the family? What if men of genius were encouraged by suitable rewards to give us good systems of education? When a man has taught a public school for 12 or 15 years with success and applause, why not relieve him from his fatigue by a handsome pension, enabling him to confine his attention to a few select scholars? I offer these as hints only. It will not be difficult to multiply them.

It is of the utmost importance to the nation, and to the King and his ministers, that young men, to whom it may befall to serve their country in parliament, should be carefully educated, and in particular be fairly initiated in the science of politics. Were the members, in general, of the two houses expert in that science, there would be no such woful division among them as at present. A clear sight of the public good, would at least damp the vile appetite for the loaves and fishes that governs many of them. If they could not entirely approve the conduct of the minister, for what minister is always right in the popular opinion, they would admonish him in an amicable manner; and if they could not prevail, would wait patiently for a more favourable opportunity. This, indeed, would be patriotism, of which the discontented party endeavour in vain to put on the mask. It is believed, that the late Sir Robert Walpole bestowed great sums upon writers, for justifying his measures. It would be a more solid plan, to engage tutors of colleges and other teachers, to

instil

instil into their pupils a due submission to government, and to teach them this useful lesson, That the public never suffers so much from an unskilful minister, as from a factious opposition. Why not schools for teaching the science of politics, erected at the expence of the public, as schools are for teaching the art of war? Such an institution, inconsistent indeed with absolute monarchy, would suit admirably the constitution of Britain. Sure I am, that never in this island was there more occasion for such schools, than in the present time,—men venting doctrines even in parliament, subversive of order and good government, tending to corrupt the whole mass of the people, and to authorise every degree of licentiousness.

An anecdote concerning Lycurgus, made a figure in ancient Greece. He brought into an assembly of Spartans two dogs, one tame and gentle, the other wild and fierce. "Know, said he, that these dogs "are not only of the same mother, but "of the same litter. The difference of "their temper proceeds entirely from "their education, and from the different "manner of their being trained."

PARENTS! your children are not your property. They are entrusted to you by Providence, to be trained up in the principles of religion and virtue; and you are bound to fulfil the sacred trust. You owe to your Maker, obedience: you owe to your children, the making of them virtuous: you owe to your country, good citizens; and you owe to ourselves, affectionate children, who, during your gray hairs, will be your sweetest comfort and firmest support *.

IN

* Crates the philosopher, wished to be on the pinacle of the highest steeple of Athens, that he might cry aloud to the citizens, "Oh senseless generation; "how foolish are ye to heap up wealth, and yet to "neglect the education of your children, for whom "ye amass it!"

In gathering materials for this work, I have adhered strictly to the system of nature; and have given no place to any observation or conjecture, but what appeared clearly founded upon that system, upon some noted principle, feeling, or faculty. Rousseau has unhappily too much imagination to be confined within so narrow bounds: he builds castles in the air, and in vain endeavours to give them a foundation. His *Emile*, however, with all its imperfections, is a work of great genius; and he has given many hints that deserve to be prosecuted. Compare his performance with others on the same subject, and its superiority will appear in a striking light. Compare it with a book intitled, *Instructions for educating a Daughter*, attributed, I must believe unjustly, to an excellent writer, the most virtuous of men, Fenelon Archbishop of Cambray. The following passage will by contrast, do honour to my favourite author. " The
" substance

" fubftance of the brain is in children
" foft and tender; but it hardens every
" day. By this foftnefs, every thing is
" eafily imprinted on it. It is not only
" foft but moift, which being joined with
" a great heat, give the child a continual
" inclination to move, whence proceeds
" the agitation of children, who are no
" more able to fix their mind on any one
" object, than their body in any one
" place. The firft images, engraven while
" the brain is foft, are the deepeft, and
" harden as age dries the brain, and con-
" fequently become indefaceable by time.
" Hence it is, that when old, we remem-
" ber many things done in youth, and not
" what were done in riper age; becaufe
" the brain at that age is dried and filled
" with other images. But if in child-
" hood, the brain be adapted for recei-
" ving images, it is not altogether fo for
" the regular difpofal of them, or for rea-
" foning. For though the moifture of

" the

" the brain renders the impreſſions eaſy,
" yet, by being joined with too great a
" heat, it makes a ſort of agitation which
" breaks the ſeries of rational deducti-
" ons." What a rant is this; words without any meaning! Here, man is reduced to be a mere machine, every thing explained from ſoft and hard, moiſt and dry, hot and cold; cauſes that have no imaginable connection with the effects endeavoured to be explained. Books of this kind may be pored on without end, and the reader be not a jot the wiſer. Why from the ſame principles, does not this moſt profound philoſopher deduce the light of the ſun, the circulation of the blood; or, what is no leſs difficult, the mathematical regularity of an egg?

EPISODE

Episode upon the Duty of Women to Nurse their own Children.

Nature has divided the human race into two sexes, male and female, which in a cursory view appear much alike; but upon a closer inspection, there are perceived many differences. The male in particular is better fitted for labour and for field-exercises: the female is better fitted for sedentary occupation and for domestic concerns. But remarkable it is, that these differences, far from breeding discord, prove to be the very cement that joins a male and a female in the closest union. In a word, the purest and most lasting happiness that human beings can attain in this life, is derived from the union of a concordant pair in the matrimonial state. Behold here the benevolence of the Deity.—He compels them in a manner

ner to accept of this bleffing, by directing in every country an equal number of male and female births, and by over-ruling with a fteady hand an infinity of repugnant chances.

The beauty of this providential fyftem and its conformity to human nature, will beft appear by oppofing it to polygamy. In it the hufband and wife, equal in dignity, are fitted by their nature for different parts in domeftic government; but with no greater authority in the male, than what is neceffary in every fociety compofed of two perfons, fuppofing them to be of the fame fex. Their mutual regard and their views being the fame, their union is complete. Polygamy on the contrary is contradictory to human nature, by banifhing equality between the fexes. It raifes the man above his rank, to have abfolute authority over his wives as over his flaves; and it degrades them below

their

their rank to be mere instruments of sensual pleasure.

Supposing now pairing in the matrimonial state to be a destination of Providence and a law of nature, the different vocations of husband and wife may be clearly ascertained from the difference of their character. The man, vigorous and active, provides for the family. The woman, more delicate and sedentary, takes care of matters within doors, nurses their offspring, and educates them during their childhood. These are primary duties founded on human nature, and by the moral sense declared indispensable. Nor are the sanctions of rewards and punishments omitted here, more than in other primary duties. Their performance is attended with self-approbation and with esteem from every one. And as for punishment, no man ever neglected his family, nor a woman her children, whose conscience

conscience was not wrung with remorse, beside being contemned by all the world. Nor is any thing omitted that belongs to the character of a primary duty. As our Maker never requires from us as a duty any particular but what antecedently is agreeable, he has made the performance of these family-duties the sweetest pleasures of life.

MORE particularly upon the duty of the mother to nurse her own children. This is a duty of too great importance to rest upon the conviction of reason merely. By a signal destination of Providence, milk is made to flow into the breasts of the mother immediately after delivery, evidently to feed her infant. A wonderful fact! which would be held by all as miraculous, did not its frequency render it familiar. As this fact is inexplicable from natural causes, it must be resolved into the immediate operation of

E   the

the Deity; and confequently it is a declaration no lefs clear of our Maker's will, than if by an angel from heaven he had declared THAT THE MOTHER'S MILK BELONGS TO HER INFANT. Nor does Providence ftop there. The neglect of this facred duty, befide remorfe, feldom efcapes bodily punifhment. The fuppreffion of milk occafions a fever, which is always dangerous, and fometimes fatal. On the other hand, a woman at no time enjoys more health, than when obeying the dictates of nature in feeding her infant with her own milk.

FROM this the following confequence neceffarily follows, that as milk is beftowed without diftinction upon every mother, Providence affuredly, with refpect to the duty of nurfing, makes no diftinction between high and low, rich and poor.

In the first stage of society when men lived chiefly on what was caught in hunting, the family-duties above delineated were unavoidable. As all men were equal, and laboured only for themselves, there was no person to undertake any duty for another. Commerce indeed and riches having introduced different modes of living, the sanctions mentioned have become more necessary than they were originally. But as human nature continues the same, and these sanctions continue in force, the family-duties of husband and wife must equally continue to be binding.

The duty of a woman to nurse her own infant is made so agreeable by nature, that even the most delicate court lady would take delight in it, were not her manners corrupted by idleness and dissipation. It is true, that the fatigue of living constantly in public, ought to be avoided during the time of nursing; nor would

would it be proper that the mother should precipitate herself into deep gaming, which might inflame her blood, and render her milk an unwholesome nourishment. She need not however sequestrate herself from the public during nursing. Moderate amusement is not only consistent with that kindly occupation, but in reality is favourable to it, by keeping her chearful and in good humour, the very best tone of mind for nursing. Nor upon the whole would she suffer, by relaxing a little during that period from the high career of diversions. On the contrary, she would return to the public with more enjoyment than any person feels who is constantly engaged.

Relative to this subject, there is a beautiful passage in Rousseau's Emile, which in English may run thus. " Of " all the branches of education, that " which is bestowed on infants is the " most

" moſt important; and that branch in-
" conteſtibly is the province of the fe-
" male ſex. Had the Author of nature
" intended it for the male ſex, he would
" have given milk to fathers for nou-
" riſhing their infants. Let treatiſes
" therefore upon education, be addreſ-
" ſed always to the women, as a mark
" of preference; for not only does
" that branch of education fall more
" naturally to them, but they are alſo
" more intereſted in it, as widows gene-
" rally depend more or leſs on their chil-
" dren. Laws, which have peace more
" in view than virtue, give not ſufficient
" authority to mothers. And yet their
" duties are more toilſome, their cares
" more important to good order, and their
" attachment to their children greater.
" There are circumſtances that in ſome
" meaſure may excuſe the want of reſpect
" to a father; but if in any circumſtance
" whatever a child is ſo unnatural as to
" be

"be deficient in refpect to the mother "who bore him, who nourifhed him with "her milk, who, for years, neglecting "herfelf, was occupied entirely about "him, he ought to be extirpated from "the earth as a monfter unworthy to "live."

THE natural affection a woman has to her child begins before birth; and grows more and more vigorous in the courfe of nurfing. Now, when a woman gives her child to be nurfed by another, has it no influence upon her, that the natural affection of her child may be transferred from her to the nurfe? And has it no influence on her, that the natural affection fhe bears her child, may decay and vanifh when it is nurfed at a diftance and is feldom in her fight?

LUXURY, which in manifold inftances has occafioned a depravation of manners,

prevails

prevails upon women of condition, to lay the burden of nursing their children upon mercenaries. A poor woman has some excuse for undertaking the charge of another woman's child, at the risk of her own. The offer of a great bribe and the favour of a great family, are to her irresistible temptations. But what has the tempter to plead who surrenders her infant to a mercenary, and suffers luxury and avidity of pleasure to prevail over natural affection? Few women would have the effrontery to shew their face in public after so gross a neglect of their offspring, were they not kept in countenance by example and fashion.

Nor is this all. The guilt of a woman who behaves in that manner, is aggravated by tempting another woman to commit the same crime. The woman who is tempted, is undoubtedly guilty; and the tempter partakes of her guilt.
However

However evident this truth may be, yet I suspect that it will make little impression upon those who, fonder of pleasure than of their children, can without reluctance abandon their new born infant to a mercenary. Nor will a woman of such a character be much affected with the risk of losing the affection of her child.

But after all, is there no danger that a low creature who has sacrificed her own infant for money, will not venture next to sacrifice the infant trusted to her, in hopes of a second bribe from another family? I have heard of such infernal practice in the great city of London. Nor ought this to be surprising. What better is to be expected of a woman who has shown herself so unkindly, or rather unnatural, to her own child? An infant of a noble family was thus reduced to extremity by wilful bad treatment; and was at the brink of the grave, when the horrid fcene was laid open by an intercepted letter from the nurfe to her hufband, acquainting him of the approaching death of the child, and defiring him to get her employed as a nurfe in fome rich family. She was turned out of doors with infamy; and the infant with difficulty was reftored to health by another nurfe. The London ladies were alarmed; and for a time thought of nurfing their own children. But the alarm vanifhed like a dream; and the practice goes on as formerly.

SUPPOSING the perfons of condition who can hire nurfes, to amount but to a hundredth part of the people, which in Britain may be 10,000, what becomes of the infants of the mercenaries? Their beft refource is in perfons ftill more needy than themfelves, willing to undertake the fuckling of thefe infants along with their own;

own; and to supply with spoon meat the deficiency of milk. Children so nursed have but a slender chance for life. Were an account taken, I should not be surprised to hear that more than the half of them die in infancy. Here is another aggravation of the guilt incurred by a woman who deviates from the law of nature, and refuses to nurse her own child.

To one ignorant of the world it must be astonishing, that so gross a breach of a fundamental law of nature should have become so general. It commenced probably in opulent cities where luxury and love of pleasure are predominant. It has descended gradually to the lower ranks; and at present few women are ashamed of it who have money to bestow on a nurse. The practice goes on smoothly; because no person is hurt but the infant, unconscious of its bad treatment. But

were

were the veil of example and fashion withdrawn, this horrid abuse would appear in its genuine colours, even to the guilty. Let us reflect but a moment upon the consequences. What can be expected from suppressing the dearest ties of natural affection, other than relaxation of manners, and a total neglect of family concerns. As the internal management of a family is the province of the wife, a woman must lay aside every regard to reputation, who can dedicate her whole time to routs, assemblies, balls, and other such giddy pleasures. She must be hardened indeed in bad habits, if the spectre of a neglected family never haunt her in her dreams, nor give her remorse when awake. Let us next turn to the husband. As no comfort is afforded to him at home, he seeks for it abroad; falls into drinking, gaming, or cohabiting with loose women; and, instead of being a useful member of society, becomes a pest in it. I cannot fet this picture in a ftronger light, than by oppofing it to that of a regular family. A woman who fuckles her child, finds not only her chief occupation at home, but her chief amufement. She relifhes the comforts of domeftic life, and communicates her fatisfaction to her hufband, to her children, and to all around her. Her family concerns are kept in order, œconomy ftudied, peace and concord eftablifhed. The hufband has no comfort any where equal to what he feels at home. Inftead of wafting his means in riot and intemperance, he ftudies with ardour to fecure a competency for his beloved wife and children. His benevolence is extended to his friends and neighbours, and to his countrymen in general. As on the one hand, nothing tends more than loofenefs of manners to enervate a ftate; fo on the other, a ftate is always found in vigour when good order and proper management

ment are preserved in families. When such are the manners of a people, dissipation is excluded: luxury indeed may creep in, but its progress will be exceedingly slow.

Upon the whole, I am acquainted with no law more anxiously enforced by natural rewards and punishments, than that which binds women of all ranks to nurse their own children: nor am I acquainted with many laws that tend more to prevent depravation of manners. The neglect of this important duty, cannot be justified nor even excused, but from want of milk or want of health.

If rational conviction need any support from authority, I have a most respectable authority at hand, namely Archbishop Tillotson, who in one of his sermons delivers the following opinion: " The duty
" of nursing their young ones is implant-
" ed

" ed by nature in all living creatures;
" and there cannot be a greater reproach
" to creatures endued with reason, than
" to neglect a duty to which nature di-
" rects even the brute creation. This
" natural duty is of a more necessary and
" indispensable obligation than any po-
" sitive precept of revealed religion; the
" neglect of which, as much as any sin
" whatsoever, is evidently a punishment
" to itself in the palpable ill effects and
" consequences of it."

LOOSE

Authority of Parents.

THE faculty of reason is bestowed on man for controlling his appetites and passions, and for giving them a proper direction. This faculty is indeed born with us; but as it is feeble like those of the body during the first stage of life, parental authority governs in its stead during that period. And, as no work of God is left imperfect, children are directed by instinct to obey their parents; and if children be not unkindly treated, their obedience is not only voluntary, but affectionate. This is not a picture of imagination: every one who has given attention to the infant state, will bear witness, that

that a child clings to its mother, and is fonder of her than of all the world beside. By this admirable syftem, children, who have no reason, are commonly better governed, than adult persons who possess a considerable share of it: the former are entirely obsequious to the reason of another; the latter not always to their own.

That the authority of parents must be absolute, is evident; because in the nature of things, it cannot be subject to any control. And it is equally evident, that the same authority must be transferred to the keeper, where the parents are dead or at a distance. But much art and delicacy are requisite in the manner of exercising it. I absolutely prohibit severity; which will render the child timid, and introduce a habit of dissimulation, the worst of habits. If such severity be exercised as to alienate the child's affection,

tion, there is an end to education; the parent or keeper is transformed into a cruel tyrant over a trembling flave. Beware, on the other hand, of bewraying any uneafinefs in refufing what a child calls for unreafonably: perceiving your uneafinefs, it will renew its attempt, hoping to find you in better humour. Even infants, fome at leaft, are capable of this artifice. Therefore, if an infant explain by figns what it ought to have, let it be gratified inftantly with a cheerful countenance. If it defire what it ought not to have, let the refufal be fedate, but firm. Regard not its crying: it will foon give over, if not liftened to. The tafk is eafier with a child who underftands what is faid to it: fay only with a firm tone, that it cannot have what it defires; but without fhewing any heat on the one hand, or concern on the other. The child, believing that the thing is impoffible, will ceafe to fret. Some children begin early to show a keenness for what touches their fancy. Lose not a moment to repress that keenness, not by bluntness or roughness, but by informing the child that it is improper. If from infancy it have been trained to obedience, it will submit pleasantly. The advantage of this discipline is not confined to childhood: it is an excellent preparation for bearing crosses and disappointments in every stage of life. How differently do the low people manage their children? If a child cry without reason, it is whipt by the angry mother; and it has now reason to cry, which it does till its little heart is like to break. The mother, still through the influence of passion, though of a different kind, melts into pity, cajoles, flatters, caresses, all to pacify the poor infant. Can any thing be more preposterous? The child soon discovers that fretting and crying will procure what it wants. As few of the lower sort ever think of disciplining their

their children to obedience, it is no wonder that there is found among them so much obstinacy and perverseness.

The absolute dependence on parents that nature puts children under, has, when rightly exercised, two effects extremely salutary. One is, that it produces a habit of submission to authority, a fine preparation for the social state. The authority of the magistrate succeeds to that of the parent; and the submission paid to the latter is readily transferred to the former. The great empire of China affords a conspicuous instance: reverence to parents is the corner-stone of that vast edifice: it is encouraged as the highest virtue; and every neglect meets disgrace and punishment. Another effect is, that the habit of submission to parental authority, introduces naturally a habit of submission to self-authority; or, in other words, a habit of submission to the authority

thority of confcience. Youth is liable to the feduction of paffion, and a dangerous period it is to thofe who have been neglected in childhood. But a young man, obedient from infancy to his parents, fubmits with as little hefitation to the dictates of his own confcience; and if happily, at his entrance into public life, he efcape temptations that are difficult to be refifted, he becomes fortified by habit to refift every temptation.

Though parental authority well tempered fits us thus for fociety and happinefs, yet that eminent writer Rouffeau, rejecting the fyftem of nature, declares for emancipating children from all fubjection, indulging them in every fancy, provided only they do no mifchief to others. I cannot really conjecture, upon what imagined principle in human nature this doctrine is founded. A child is incapable to judge for itfelf; and yet it it muſt not be directed by its parents. "Pray Sir, hold off, there ought to be no authority, the child muſt be left to itſelf." This is a ſtrange notion. Can it be improper to tell a child, that what it deſires is wrong; or that the doing what it deſires would make it deſpiſed or hated? If the child be not ſo far advanced as to underſtand that language, nothing remains but plain authority, which the child ſubmits to readily and pleaſantly. Rouſſeau maintains, that you muſt not pretend to have any authority over your pupil, but only that you are the ſtronger, and can ſubject him by force [*]. Is not this to teach him, that right depends on force; and that he may lawfully ſubject every one who is weaker than himſelf? Was it Rouſſeau's intention to breed his pupil a tyrant and oppreſſor? he could not take a more effectual method.

---

[*] Emile, vol. I. p. 95.

An infallible way of rendering a child unhappy, is to indulge it in all its demands. Its defires multiply by gratification, without ever refting fatisfied: it is lucky for the indulging parents, if it demand not the moon for a play-thing. You cannot give every thing; and your refufal diftreffes the creature more, than if you had ftopt fhort at firft. A child in pain is entitled to great indulgence: but beware of yielding to fancy; the more the child is indulged, the more headftrong it grows, and the more impatient of a difappointment.

I am acquainted with a very refpectable couple, difciples of Rouffeau; more however, I conjecture, from inclination than from conviction. They feldom hitherto have employed any means for reftraining their children, but promifes and intreaties. As the father was playing at chefs with a friend, one of his children,

Authority of Parents. 55

a boy of about four years, took a piece from the board and away to play with it. Harry, fays the father, let us have back the man, and there's an apple for you. The apple was foon devoured, and another chefs-man laid hold of. In fhort, they were obliged to fufpend the game, till the boy, turning hungry, was led away to fupper. I would have fuch parents confider, whether they are not here mifled by felf-deceit. Their motive they imagine is tendernefs for their poor babes. But the real motive is their own weaknefs, which they indulge at the expence of their babes; for muft it not even to them be evident, that to indulge irregular fancies in creatures deftitute of reafon, is to inveft fancy with abfolute authority, and to dethrone virtue. It perhaps will be obferved, that this cafe falls not under the general rule, being an inftance of a child by its petulance hurting others. If fo, what is laid down as a general rule, muft must be contracted within narrower limits. But, letting that pass, what would our author have said upon the following case. A gentleman, upon a visit at a friend's house, heard little master crying below stairs. The mother alarmed was told, that he wanted to ride up to table upon the roast beef, and that the cook did not relish the project. The mother was for letting Dickie have his will. But the father luckily reflected, that the sirloin would probably be too hot a seat for Dickie. Rousseau would have made this also an exception, as he could not mean, that parents should stand by and suffer their children to hurt themselves. His doctrine thus reformed, resolves in giving children full liberty in matters indifferent, such as can neither hurt themselves nor others; to which restriction I willingly subscribe. And thus a doctrine ushered in with solemnity as a leading principle in the education of children, and

and seeming at first view of great importance, does, upon a more narrow infpection, vanifh into fmoke.

HAVING difcuffed authority, the corner-ftone as it were of the building, my aim was to have ftated the following hints in ftrict order; but in vain. And after all, what order can be expected in loofe hints? All I can undertake is to arrange them fo as to correfpond to the different ftages of nonage, the fimpleft firft, the more complex after; to be put in practice when the mind is ready for them.

SECT. II.

MANAGEMENT of CHILDREN in the First Stage of Life.

IN a complete treatise upon education of children, every principle, every instinct, every passion, and every appetite ought to be carefully dissected. But this is far beyond my purpose, and I suspect beyond my reach. I venture only to give instructions upon such of the particulars above mentioned, as display themselves early, and make some figure even in childhood. A fair commencement of a subject, mostly new, is all I pretend to. May I not indulge the pleasing hope, that a subject of so great importance will be ripened by others, and perhaps brought to perfection by the ablest hands. The following instructions belong to the present section.

1*st*, A POWER to recal at will pleasing objects, would be a greater blessing than ever was bestowed in a fairy tale. The pleasure of health is little felt, except in its absence: it is however a real blessing; not only as it is a security against pain, but as it naturally suggests pleasing objects. In the latter respect, however, it is inferior to cheerfulness and sweetness of temper; which are not only in themselves pleasant, but still more by directing the mind to none but agreeable objects. A sullen and morose temper, on the contrary, is not only in itself unpleasant, but still more by calling to mind no objects but what are disagreeable.

This observation may be turned to good account in education. Do we wish to make our children happy? Let them be accustomed to agreeable objects, and a veil drawn over those that are disagreeable

agreeable. Cheerfulness and agreeable objects, have a mutual influence: the former attracts the latter; and the latter by reaction invigorate the former. Can any one doubt, that fettering infants new born in folds of linen, which they struggle against in vain, must have an effect upon their temper? Were that treatment long continued, it would produce a lasting habit of fretfulness. This, among other objections to the practice, is of great weight. Why should not the children of people in easy circumstances, be roused from sleep every morning with music? Why not be entertained frequently with agreeable pictures; and why not be amused with ludicrous stories to make them laugh? I would however be far from excluding subjects that excite pity and tender concern. Pity is indeed painful; but far from disagreeable, even in the actual feeling. I am pleased with myself for having sympathized

thized with another; and that pleasing reflection adds to my happiness.

AGREEABLE impressions may be made upon an infant even in its mother's womb. The mother during pregnancy ought to banish all dismal thoughts, and preserve herself as much as possible calm and cheerful. There is little doubt but that this will benefit her infant. The same reason holds for chusing a nurse or keeper of an even and cheerful temper.

A HABIT of cheerfulness acquired in infancy, contributes not a little to health. The Druids of old were eminently skilled in physic. Their chief *recipe* for preserving health was expressed in three words, *cheerfulness, temperance, exercise*. This habit contributes not less to alleviate misfortunes. It makes us see every object in its best light, and fits us to submit to accidents without repining. " Almost
" every

" every object that attracts our notice,
" has its bright and its dark side: he
" that habituates himself to look at the
" dark side, will four his disposition, and
" consequently impair his happiness;
" while he who constantly beholds the
" bright side, insensibly meliorates his
" temper, and, in consequence of it, im-
" proves his own happiness, and the hap-
" piness of all about him *."

2*d*, WILL I be thought to refine too much when I maintain, that a habit of cheerfulness acquired during infancy, will contribute to make a face beautiful? A savage mind produces savage manners; and these in conjunction produce a harsh and rugged countenance. Hence it is that a national face improves gradually, with the manners of the people. Listen to this ye mothers, with respect especially to your female children: you will find

that

* The WORLD, No. 126.

that cheerfulness is a greater beautifier than the finest pearl powder.

Some children are by nature rash and impetuous: a much greater number are shy and timid. The disposition of a child appears early; and both extremes ought to be corrected, whenever an opportunity occurs. Fear is a passion implanted in our nature, to warn us of danger, in order to guard against it. When moderate, so as to raise our activity only, without overwhelming the mind, it is a most salutary passion: but when it swells to excess, which it is apt to do in a timid disposition, far from contributing to safety, it stupifies the man, and renders him incapable of action. If your pupil therefore be of a fearful temper, you cannot begin too early to fortify him against that weakness. Most children are afraid of a new object that is formidable in its appearance, a large dog for example.

Handle

Handle it familiarly, and show it to be harmless: the child will be perſuaded to do the ſame. A child, as Rouſſeau obſerves, is afraid of a maſk. Begin with ſhowing it an agreeable maſk: put it on laughing; others laugh, and the child laughs. Accuſtom the child to maſks leſs and leſs agreeable: it will in time be afraid of no maſk, however ugly. Thunder has an awful ſound, and is apt to raiſe fear. Lead your pupil to the fields when it thunders: it will in time ceaſe to fear. Guard your children with unremitting care againſt tales of ghoſts and hobgoblins, which in childhood make a deep impreſſion. As ſuch tales are always connected with darkneſs, accuſtom your children to grope their way in the dark. Rouſſeau's method of teaching children to act in the dark, deſerves to be imitated. I was told by a lady of rank, that by engaging her ſervants to follow her example, ſuch tales were unknown

known in her family. Her children were trained to say their prayers in a dark room, after receiving the following inftruction, " Thy Father which feeth in " fecret will reward thee openly." They were difciplined to lay up their playthings in fuch order, as to find them readily in the dark.

WITH refpect to the oppofite extreme of rafhnefs and impetuofity, lay hold of every proper opportunity for moderating it; and there is little doubt of fuccefs, if proper means be ufed. Sometimes even an accident will affift: a child happening to fall down a few fteps of a ftair, it for fome time would neither go up nor down without its maid. There is no occafion to warn children againft feen danger: no child is ever difpofed to throw itfelf down from a window, nor to jump into a fierce running ftream. But there are things that attract the eye by their luftre, which an infant will endeavour to grasp, because it sees no danger; a burning candle for example, or a shining knife. Teach your infant to guard against such things: put your hand once or twice on a silver boiler full of hot water, and draw it away with signs of pain. After putting the infant's hand on it till it feels pain, let it understand by signs that the thing ought not to be touched. This will have its proper effect, even before the infant can speak. An infant endeavours to grasp the blade of a knife, being the shining part. Cut its finger cunningly till the blood appear. Let it understand by signs that this is done by the knife: it will avoid a knife till it learn to handle it without danger. A lady made the experiment on an infant of a year; and it not only avoided the knife, but looked concerned when others handled it. At the age of six or seven, boys, in imitation of men, will attempt things above their strength.

strength. In that case, it is proper to restrain them by pointing out the danger.

3*d*, CHILDREN are prone to complain, because they have no power to right themselves. Complaints too readily listened to, will set children of a family at variance with one another. Disregard a slight complaint, and admonish the complainer, that it ought to love its brother or sister, instead of bringing it to punishment by complaining. If the complaint deserve a hearing, receive it coolly, and say that enquiry shall be made. Admonish the offender privately to give satisfaction, particularly by instant restitution, if it have taken any thing from the complainer. This way of redressing wrongs, instead of raising enmity, may contribute to cordiality among the children of a family.

4*th*, IF proper authority be maintained from the beginning, stubbornness in a child

child will be a vice unknown; but if laid aside or relaxed, stubbornness soon appears in some children. Mr Locke mentions a lady whose daughter was nursed in the country. She found the child so stubborn, as to be forced to whip it eight times before it was subdued. This was the first and the last time of laying a hand upon it. Ever after, it was all compliance and obedience. This ought to be a lesson to parents never to relax the reins of government. Doubtless the mother here suffered more pain than the child. Consult Rousseau's method of subduing an obstinate boy*.

5*th*, MAN is an imitative being; and his proneness to imitation may be made subservient to good culture. A child under three, shrinks from every grown person, except those of its acquaintance. But it is fond of children. Let

* Emile, vol. I. p. 149.

a child of six or seven, carefully educated, associate with younger children, they will learn more by imitation than by much verbal instruction. Even before infants can speak, they understand by signs your disapprobation of a fretful person, or of one who is dirty and slovenly. But imitation is a two-edged weapon: though nature dictates to boys and girls different amusements, yet nature may be warped by circumstances. A boy educated with girls of his own age, will imitate their manners, and become effeminate. In this part of the world, it is more common to see a girl imitate the manners of the boys with whom she is educated. Such wrong biasses ought to be guarded against. There are instances of persons having contracted a bad manner of speaking, from hearing daily the inarticulate sounds of the younger part of the family. Nature, indeed, directs us to imitate those above us; but a child of six or seven, living with

with several younger, will descend to partake of their amusements, rather than be left alone.

6*th*, A favourite child, indulged by its parents to assume authority over others, will become a tyrant when grown up. Some children are disposed to treat servants with haughtiness and contempt. If this temper in children be not repressed, they will become like negro-drivers in our colonies, or our carters at home. Give authority to your servants to let such children know, that they are not their servants, nor owe them obedience. From this treatment they will discover, that civility and intreaty, are the only means for procuring what they want.

7*th*, THAT in the nature of some individuals, there is a disposition to cruelty, cannot be disguised, being evident from various facts. Strong symptoms of it appear

pear in childhood, during which period there is nothing hid. It is not uncommon in a child, after careffing its favourite puppy, to kick and beat it; or, after ſtroking its ſparrow, to pull off its head. I have ſeen a little girl, after ſpending hours in dreſſing its doll, throw it over the window in a ſudden fit. This diſeaſe is not eaſily cured, becauſe, like the King's evil, it is kept ſecret. I know of no cure ſo effectual, as to enure a child of this temper to objects of pity and concern. Such objects frequently preſented, and at proper times, may give a turn to the diſtemper, and make it yield to humanity. Such fits of cruelty however, are far from being general. There are many children, who, having no malice in their compoſition, are invariably kind to their favourites, and charitable to perſons in want.

8*th*, It is a capital point to enure young perſons to ſuffer accidental evils with firmneſs.

firmnefs. Children at play, bear ftrokes, fatigue, and hunger, without repining; and cuftom will render fuch evils familiar and eafy. This was held an important branch of education among the Spartans; witnefs the young man who fuffered a fox he had ftolen to eat into his bowels, rather than difclofe the theft. The feat of pain is in the mind; and accordingly bodily diftrefs is felt much the lighter when the mind is prepared for it. If a child cut its finger or get a bump on its head by a fall, it foftens the pain to make a joke of it, to laugh, and to make the child laugh. If it fall a crying, fay " that it is below a perfon of fafhion " to mind a fall, that no children cry " but beggars brats, and that fuch a one " fuffered more without complaining." Nurfes and fervants increafe the child's diftrefs, by an appearance of pity and concern. Death commonly is very little painful: the pain lies in the imagination of the dying perſon, raiſed by the tears and melancholy looks of the attendants. Teach a boy to ſuffer ſlight pain without concern, and he will become a hero. If too careful to prevent pain, you render your child a coward.

THIS branch of education is for the moſt part ill conducted, eſpecially among the lower ranks. A child, ſlipping a foot and falling, cries from fear more than from pain. It is whipped for crying, though no antecedent care had been taken to correct that weakneſs. It cries bitterly; and now every thing muſt be done to appeaſe the poor child. The floor is beat for hurting babie: it gets a ſugar-plum to give over crying. Such treatment inculcates more than one bad leſſon. The beating of the floor foſters revenge in the child. The ſugar-plum teaches it to cry when it wants any thing; and hence artifice and ſimulation.

9*th*, THAT cleanliness proceeds from an internal sense, is made evident in Sketches of the History of Man *. This sense, originally weak like many others, is capable of being fortified by education. Let every thing be clean about your children: give signs of disgust at a dirty hand or a dirty frock, of which even an infant before it can speak, will comprehend the meaning. I was informed by a lady, not a little studious of human nature, that a child of hers, not two years old, seeing a dirty spot on her frock, cut it out, knowing no better way of removing the eye-sore.

* Edit. 2. vol. I. p. 320.

SECT.

SECT. III.

Management *of* Children *in their Second Stage.*

1*ſt*, Hesiod, a Greek Poet, than whom we know none more ancient, makes the following inſtructive obſervation, that the gods invented induſtry in order to make us virtuous. Nothing indeed equals induſtry for preventing vice. Parents and tutors! apply this obſervation to the children under your care. Keep them employed, keep them buſy, and they will never have a wrong thought. Let them indulge themſelves in play as long as they incline; but draw them off when they begin to tire. Train them to do every thing for themſelves as much as poſſible; which will not only promote their activity, but excite their invention. Children who have every thing furniſhed ed to them without labour or thought on their part, will become indolent and incapable of any vigorous exertion,—helpless beings who muſt employ another hand even to buckle a ſhoe. In order to exerciſe invention, children ſhould have no play-things but what they make themſelves, or help to make. A play-thing that gratifies the ſight only, is not long reliſhed; but a child never tires of one that gives it exerciſe. A girl continues fond of her doll, being conſtantly employed in dreſſing and undreſſing it. She makes it act the viſitor in the drawing-room: ſhe makes it do the honours of the table: ſhe gives it correction and inſtruction. Such things you will ſee imitated by a girl even in her fourth year. I know not that there has been invented any ſuch play-thing for a boy of the ſame age. A bow and arrows require more years; and ſo does the art of walking blindfold in a ſtraight line, or of ſearching for any thing in the dark. Running for a prize is an exercife too violent for boys of twice that age. Riding on a ſtick is fo faint an imitation of riding on horfe-back, as not to be long relifhed. For want of fuitable play-things, employ them in matters that require fome thought. Send your fon to bring you the ripeſt apple in the garden, or the number of fruit-trees that cover the wall, or of horfes in a certain inclofure. Send him to borrow for you fuch a book; or to make your apology for breaking an appointment. Hide a pen-knife in a fcritore: fend him to bring it. If unfuccefsful, fend him again, and he finds it at laſt. This will exercife both his induſtry and invention. Set things before him for a choice, a picture-book, a pair of gloves, filver buckles, a child's bow and arrows. Demand a reafon for his choice, which will give you occafion to inſtruct him about a right choice. Employ your daughter the fame same way, especially in matters that belong more properly to her sex. I am told, that there is an English boarding school, in which the girls have gardening for an amusement. A certain spot is allotted to each, which she fills with flowers, and weeds with a hoe accommodated to her size.

There are other exercises fitted for boys as well as girls, which I introduce here for the sake of connection, though perhaps the next section may be thought a more proper place for them. To initiate children in the knowledge of trees, of fruit, and of their names, take a leaf from each of the common kinds, an oak, a beech, an elm, &c. Spread them on a table, and point out to your pupils the particulars that difference each of them from the rest. Add from time to time leaves of trees less common. Your pupils will

will learn to know every tree at firſt ſight by its leaf. This is a fine introduction to botany, and a promoter of it. An apricot, a peach, a nectarine, are readily diſtinguiſhable; but to diſtinguiſh the different kinds of apples and of pears, and to give names to each, requires more labour than is commonly given. And this may be made an amuſement even for children of four or five. Show them the different kinds, and point out the peculiarities of ſhape and colour. The young creatures will be fond of this exerciſe, and will ſoon be expert in it. Such exerciſes have the double advantage of ſerving for inſtruction as well as for paſtime. Another amuſement will ſerve as an early introduction to hiſtory. Collect prints of eminent perſons, ancient and modern. After examining a print with attention, give a ſhort account of the perſon it repreſents, Epaminondas for example, who delivered his country from Spartan

Spartan oppreffion, or Julius Cæfar, who enflaved his country. Proceed at intervals to other prints, with proper obfervations for improving your pupils in virtuous principles, and for giving them a diftafte to vice. When fufficiently ripe, let them take the lead, and one after another, name the perfons and their hiftory who are reprefented in the prints. Entering into a courfe of hiftory in more advanced years, they will have double pleafure in renewing their acquaintance with the perfons who make the chief figure.

INDUSTRY produces many other good effects. In the *firft* place, an induftrious perfon is always in good humour. Labouring people never tire, becaufe they have always fomething to do. To languifh for want of occupation, is the envied lot of the opulent; their amufements by familiarity foon turning infipid. Women of fortune having nothing to animate them after the vanities of youth are over, become vapourish and unhappy. In the *next* place, a habit of application smooths the road to schools and colleges; and makes it easy to acquire every sort of knowledge. Nothing on the other hand is more baneful, than a habit of sauntering. This is easily prevented in children, because they are naturally active; but with difficulty after the habit is begun. The neglect of this material article, has proved the ruin of many a hopeful genius: it is little less faulty, than the indulging of young persons in vicious habits; for idleness is an inlet to many vices.

Rousseau declares against imposing tasks on children. I cannot help differing. Children are fond to be employed. Let their tasks at first be agreeable, and much within their ability; time and habit will enable them to overcome the most

moſt difficult.. This ſort of culture, is at any rate neceſſary for preparing a young man to learn a trade. How indocile in the hand of a maſter muſt the apprentice be, who has always been permitted to act without reſtraint!

2*d*, WHAT comes next in order, is to promote every virtue in your children, of which benevolence is the capital. The man who is fond of his own ſweet perſon, and of his own little pleaſures, has no reliſh of benevolence, nor money to ſpare upon others. On the other hand, he who ſpares upon himſelf, is commonly liberal to thoſe he is connected with. Pliny the younger was famous for doing good. He paid the debts of one, portioned the daughter of another, gave his nurſe a bit of land for her ſuſtenance, made an eſtabliſhment for orphans and poor children,—all upon a very moderate income. To one curious to know the fund that
ſupported

supported so much expence, he answered simply, " What is wanting of yearly rent " is supplied by frugality." The late Earl of Elgin, permitted his two sons in their hours of play, to associate with boys in the neighbourhood; which he thought better, than to expose them to be corrupted at home by his servants, filling them with notions of their rank and quality. One day, the two boys being called to dinner, a young lad, their companion, said, " I'll wait till you return, as there " is no dinner for me at home. Have " you no money to buy it ? No. Come " then and dine with us. No." " Papa," says the eldest, " what was the price of " the silver buckles you gave me ? Five " shillings. Let me have them, and I'll " give you the buckles." It was done accordingly. The Earl, enquiring privately, found that the money was given to the lad. The buckles were returned, and the boy was highly commended for

being

being kind to his companion. A crowd of boys, difmiffed from the grammar fchool on a Saturday, attacked a beggar who was in liquor, pelting him with dirt and ftones for their diverfion. One only there was, who did every thing to make his companions defift. He applied to a woman who kept a ftall hard by, offering all the money he had, if fhe would refcue the poor creature. The woman, admiring the boy's humanity, told the ftory to his mother's cook, from whom it afcended to the parlour. The mother was delighted: but the boy, afraid that his companions would hold him in derifion for fuch weaknefs, threatned revenge againft the woman. The mother laid hold of the opportunity to convince her fon, that it was fhameful to abufe a poor creature who could not defend himfelf; and that the lads would be chaftifed by their parents, for doing a thing fo unworthy of gentlemen; exhorting him to
perfevere

persevere in what was right, without regarding his companions. A boy about the age of ten, says to his father, " Papa, " give me some money. There is a shil- " ling, will that do? No." " There's a " guinea. Thank you papa." The gentleman discovered, that it was given to a woman who had been delivered of twins, and was obliged to hire a nurse for one of them. A boy of five years, observing that a gentleman playing at cards did not pay what he lost, and concluding that he had no money, begged some from his father to give to the gentleman. A boy between seven and eight, of a noble family, strayed accidentally into a hut, where he saw a poor woman with a sick child on her knee. Struck with compassion, he instantly gave her all the money he had; carried to her from the herb market, turnips and potatoes, with bread and scraps from his father's kitchen. The parents enchanted with their son, took
the

the poor family off his hand. Two or three years after, he saved the whole of his weekly allowance, till it amounted to eleven or twelve shillings, and purchased a Latin dictionary, which he sent to a comrade of his at the grammar school. Many other acts of goodness are recorded of this boy in the family. Can there be conceived a misfortune that will sink deeper into the heart of affectionate parents, than the death of such a child? It wrings my heart to think of it.

> Ostendent terris hunc tantum fata, neque ultra
> Esse sinent.
> Heu, miserande puer! si qua fata aspera rumpas,
> Tu MARCELLUS eris.

THERE is no branch of education more neglected than the training of young persons to be charitable. And yet were this virtue instilled into children, susceptible of deep impressions, a legal provision for the poor would be rendered unnecessary: it would relieve England from the poor rates,

rates, a grievous burden that undermines both induſtry and morals. Give to each of your children a ſmall ſum for charity. Let them account to you for the difpofal; and to the child who has made the moſt judicious diſtribution, give double the ſum, to be laid out in the ſame way. It is not my opinion, that a child's liberality ſhould be repaid with intereſt, which Mr Locke adviſes, ſect. 110; for this would encourage covetouſneſs, not benevolence.

THE practice of doing good, cannot fail to improve a benevolent diſpoſition. Occupy your pupil in relieving the indigent, not only by his purſe, but by kindly offices. Convince him that he cannot be more honourably employed.

COMPASSION may be envigorated in a young mind, by a ſight of objects in diſtreſs. But beware of making ſuch objects

objects too familiar, which would blunt compassion, instead of envigorating it. Priests and physicians, being employed much about dying persons, have commonly little concern but to do their duty.

INSTRUCT your pupils that they owe civility to all, and that civility to the poor will procure them more good-will, than civility to the rich. Civility to the latter may be understood flattery: civility to the former can have no cause but humanity.

3*d*, GRATITUDE is one of the laws of nature, to which we are strictly bound; and children should be trained to be grateful, as much as to be just. Benevolence and gratitude are finely connected: a kindly office excites gratitude; and the expectation of a grateful return, is a spur to kindness and benevolence. Two elderly ly ladies in the neighbourhood of Edinburgh, who were in eafy circumftances though not in affluence, took a liking to a poor boy in the village, and gave him an invitation to their kitchen when hungry. They put him to a country fchool, and defrayed the expence of his education. He left the fchool to go abroad; and the firft account they heard of him, after an interval of many years, was a fettlement upon them of an annuity of L. 50 to each for life. By this time one of the ladies was dead, and the furvivor enjoys to this day the whole L. 100. This is a pregnant inftance of the principle of gratitude planted by nature in the human heart, a moft fhining virtue, if not the moft important in fociety. Let parents and tutors advert to this benign influence of nature. And if they apply to its cultivation, they feldom will be unfuccefsful.

4th, CURIOSITY is an appetite implanted in man for acquiring knowledge. Children have it in perfection; for to them every thing is new and unknown. They are constantly asking questions; which ought to be answered according to their capacity: to neglect their questions, or to laugh at them, shows great ignorance of the principles of education; for to give satisfaction to children by answering their questions, has a direct tendency to enlighten their minds. The answer to one question suggests commonly a second; and the ingenuity that some children show in such questions, is truly surprising. Such correspondence between parent and child, tends also to increase their mutual affection: the parent is pleased with the child's appetite for knowledge; and the child is fond of its parent for listening to it. " Knowledge," says Locke, " is grateful to the understand-" ing, as light is to the eyes. Children

" are

" are delighted when their enquiries are
" regarded, and their defire of knowledge
" encouraged and commended."

STRONGER evidence there can be none of man's difpofition for fociety, than the curiofity all have about the character and conduct of their fellow-creatures. The fondnefs of children for ftories ought to be laid hold of, as a mean no lefs pleafing than effectual, for making virtuous impreffions that never wear out. A collection of proper ftories feparated into claffes that are adapted to different ages, would be a valuable acquifition to the public. The firft clafs, fitted for children of four or five, fhould contain fhort ftories, exhibiting fimple pictures of virtue and vice, expreffed in the plaineft terms. The fecond clafs, adapted to the age of fix or feven, fhould contain ftories of the fame kind, a little more complicated. Let the third contain regular ftories, difplaying

the

the good confequences of virtue, and the bad confequences of vice, ftill in a fimple ftile. Here is room for the tutor, to inculcate more fully thefe different confequences. This clafs is proper to children from nine to eleven. In the fourth clafs, the ftile may be raifed and refined; and ftories felected that afford a ftriking moral; or in other words, that fhow not only the beauty, but the advantage of virtue; not only the deformity, but the mifchief of vice. The laft clafs, fit for the finifhing ftage of education, may be of complicated ftories in various ftiles, preferring what have the moft obvious moral. This clafs may be eafily filled with a felection from the numberlefs ftories of that kind already in print. Such inftructions, if made a daily work, would be a great improvement, by ftamping on the mind virtuous impreffions, at a time when it is the moft fufceptible of impreffions. They would alfo ripen the judgment, by

inuring

enuring the youth of both sexes, to think and reason upon causes and consequences. When absurd stories of ghosts and apparitions make so deep impressions, without having any foundation in nature, have we not reason to believe, that impressions equally deep, may be made by stories of benevolence, gratitude, friendship, parental and filial affection, and of other virtues which have a solid foundation in nature? I think it is Mr Addison who observes, that the benevolence of the English peasants, is partly owing to the simple, but celebrated ballad, *The Babes of the Wood*. The Archbishop of Cambray, had a high opinion of this sort of culture. He composed *the Adventures of Telemachus*, for the instruction of his pupil the Duke of Burgundy; and other sweet fables, which every young person is delighted with.

To fortify the impreffions made in the courfe of this culture, a fet of hiftorical prints well chofen would greatly contribute; and as this is a pleafing ftudy, it may be ufed as one of many rewards for behaving well. I give for an example, the hiftory of the Prodigal Son, carried on through feveral prints. Prepare your pupils, by relating the ftory in an interefting manner: then exhibit the prints one by one. They will be fond to examine each picture with every figure in it; and with your help, will foon be able to explain the meaning. The moft important part remains, which is, to inculcate the moral, " That children behaving " properly, will always find their parents " to be their beft friends ; and that even " when they go aftray, fincere repentance " will reftore them to favour." The ftory of Jofeph and his brethern in different prints, is another good example, not only highly interefting, but affording much

much inſtruction. Hogarth's *Good Apprentice*, exhibits an excellent moral for children; but is too complex for beginners.

5*th*, AN important object that belongs to every ſtage of education, is the diſciplining young people to reſtrain their deſires and appetites; which is not difficult, if parents begin early to exert their abſolute authority. There is great virtue in reſtraining an appetite when the temptation is ſtrong; and ſuch virtue in a young perſon, cannot be ſufficiently applauded. If a child infiſt, ſay dryly, but firmly, that it is not to be done. In more advanced years, when reaſon begins to peep out, explain the folly of it. Children by ſuch diſcipline, acquire gradually the power of ſelf-denial, highly uſeful in the conduct of life. " If the " child," ſays Mr Locke, " muſt have " grapes or ſugar-plums, when he has a " mind

" mind to them; why, when grown up,
" muſt he not be ſatisfied too, if his de-
" ſires carry him to wine or women?
" He who is not uſed to ſubmit his will
" to the reaſon of others while he is
" young, will ſcarce hearken or ſubmit
" to his own reaſon when he is of an age
" to make uſe of it." A paſſion directed to a particular object; a beautiful female for example, ſoon exhauſts itſelf by its violence. An appetite that can be gratified different ways, ſuch as ambition or avarice, may laſt for ever. In the courſe of education, appetites of that ſort ought to be checked with ſolicitude: if they once get a ſeat in the mind, it is vain to think of expelling them. Children are fond of things that touch the palate. After dining in their nurſery, introduce your children to the gueſts when the deſert is on the table. If a child aſk any thing, ſay dryly, " You have dined, let us dine:
" we demanded none of your victuals,
" why

"why should you have any of ours?" Renew this frequently, and your children will acquire a habit of seeing without desiring. A noble Lord, now in heaven, favoured by Providence with a family of fine children, permitted no play-thing to be given them, leaving them to invent amusements for themselves. He observed, "That children are fond of toys, especially of toys that please by their novelty; and that frequent presents to them of such things, bring on a habit of intemperate longing for trifles." Children tire the soonest of what they are the fondest, but without lessening their avidity for new things; and if these be supplied in plenty, the appetite is strengthened by habit, requiring variety in playthings, as well as beauty. This habit continues for life, with no alteration but what proceeds from age: the objects only are varied from childish toys to those of idle men. And hence the endless circle of minute pleasures, which to men of fortune become necessaries of life. You cannot begin too early, to check the desire that children have for toys and gewgaws. Take opportunity in presence of your children, to display your ornaments and fine things. Carry them sometimes to a toyshop. Make presents to persons about you: let not your children hope to get any; and they will learn in time to see such things with indifference. People do not sufficiently consider the mischievous effects of indulging children in their fancies: many men, who in their tender years had been perverted by such indulgence, have dissipated great estates upon mere trifles.

6*th*, There is no incitement for behaving well of greater efficacy, than to let your child know, that you think it worthy of being employed and trusted. A lady of high rank gave the charge of her confections

fections to her daughter, a child of four years. The child, accompanied with her maid, was punctual in executing the commiſſion; and no leſs faithful than punctual, never having once offered to purloin the ſlighteſt thing. This experiment requires, indeed, a faithful attendant: if a child, committing a breach of truſt, find that the ſecret can be kept, it will proceed in the ſame track, and the conſequence will be deplorable. A regulation in ſome boarding ſchools, of giving to an elder girl the care of two younger, for dreſſing them and giving them leſſons, is excellent. Truſt your young ſon with papers, with money, with a book, requiring him to preſerve theſe things carefully till called for.

7*th*, An article of the greateſt nicety, is to enure children to keep a ſecret. Tell your child any thing in the way of ſecrefy, not to be revealed on any account.

Have

Have a faithful servant on the watch. If you find that your child has blabbed, mention not your informer, but say, " that the secret has taken air, and that " it must have come from you. I do " not blame you much, because you are " a child; but be more on your guard " hereafter." If the secret be kept, employ a person to talk to the child, and to endeavour to draw the secret from it. If the child stand firm, say to it after an interval, " I find you have kept my secret. " You are a good child, and you shall be " my confident."

8*th*, THE notion of property arises from an innate sense, which teaches even infants to distinguish between *yours* and *mine*. It is however during infancy so faint, as in most children to yield to any vivid appetite. As society depends in a great measure on the sense of property, neglect no opportunity to fortify that sense in your children.

children. Make them sensible, that it is a great wrong to take what belongs to another. " How would you like to have " your little dog taken from you by " force? The knife you have taken is " not yours, what right have you to it? " You ought to be satisfied with your " own play-things, and not covet what " belongs to another." Let not the slightest transgression escape: it ought to be punished with shame and disgrace.

SECT. IV.

Management *of* Children *in their Third Stage.*

THE inftructions hitherto given, require in children no degree of underftanding, but what is derived from nature, before the faculty of reafon begins to be unfolded. What are contained in the prefent fection require fome fhare of that faculty; and upon that account, I term it the third ftage of childhood. Education during this ftage may be carried on, not only by facts and incidents as in the foregoing ftages, but by advice, by exhortation, by moral leffons, which require reafon on the child's part. But let thofe who prefide over education attend to the proper time for carrying on this branch. Moral leffons abftracted from facts, never make any impreffion on children,

children, unless to breed disgust. When your pupil is agitated with some incident that gives him concern, take that opportunity to lecture upon it, to show its good or bad tendency; and you will be heard with avidity. Except upon such an occasion, pure reasoning will have no good effect. Dry instruction is for men only: the wise Solomon did not intend his Proverbs for children.

The great variety of matter that comes under this section, requires it to be divided into parts, beginning with the improvement of active virtues; next, the improvement of restraining virtues; third, relative matters that fall not directly under either head, but are nearly connected with both.

1*st*, With regard to active virtues, there is a beauty in candour and plain dealing, which procures good will and affection,

affection, even above many virtues that make a more splendid figure. Nature prompts to this virtue; for no person ever recurred to diffimulation but to hide fome wrong. Candour is indeed a great fweetner in fociety, for without it there can be no friendfhip nor mutual confidence. Marifchal de Turenne, when he commanded in Germany, was offered a confiderable fum by a neutral city to march another way. " I cannot accept, " faid the Marifchal, becaufe I do not " intend to take the road to your city." This fingle ftroke of character, was fufficient to endear that great man, even to the enemies of his country: fuch candour is fcarce confiftent with any vice. As children are naturally candid, it is an eafy and pleafant tafk to keep them fo. If their confidence be gained by kindly treatment, they will never think of diffembling.

2*d*, In

2*d*, IN the foregoing section it was observed, that the way to invigorate compassion in a child, is to show it objects in distress. You may now add instruction to sight. Make your children sensible that none are secure against misfortunes, and that neither birth, health, nor riches afford protection. Give them instances of the vicissitudes of fortune, of men in high life reduced like Haman to bitter misery. Cicero, talking of Cæsar in one of his pleadings, paints in lively colours his martial atchievements, overcoming seasons as well as enemies; but mentions with more satisfaction, the generous protection he gave to an old friend, who, by an unforeseen event, had fallen not only into misery but into disgrace. " Con-
" quest, says he, makes a man immortal;
" and who would not exert every power
" to become immortal! Acts of private
" friendship can have no motive but
" goodness of heart. And considering
" Cæsar

" Cæsar at the top of human grandeur,
" continuing attentive, like a private per-
" son, to the necessities of the unhappy,
" I esteem him a greater man than in
" the midst of his victories."

3*d*, THERE cannot be a more instructive lesson to young persons, than that happiness depends not on pomp and grandeur, nor on other external circumstances. The seat of happiness is in the heart: one contented with his lot cannot be unhappy. Augustus, after prevailing over his rivals, governed during 40 years a mighty empire. His immense power, however, could not protect him from affliction. It did not prevent him from exclaiming against Varus, for the loss of his German legions; nor from beating his head against the wall, and filling his palace with lamentations. What availed his conquests, when his intimate friends plotted against his life? his grandeur did not prevent the misconduct of some of his relations, nor the death of all. He himself, the last of his family, was misled by his wife, to name a monster for his successor. Such was the miserable fate of that master of the world; though pronounced the happiest of men, by those who can pierce no deeper than the surface.

4th, TASTE is one of our faculties that is the slowest in its progress toward maturity; and yet may receive some improvement, during the course of domestic education. Compare with your pupils two poems on the same subject, or two passages. Take the lead in pointing out beauties and blemishes, in the simplest manner. After some time, let them take the lead under your correction. You cannot have a better book for that exercise than the *Spectator*. A pleasing vein of genteel humour runs through every one

of

of Addison's papers, which, like the sweet flavour of a hyacinth, constantly cheers, and never overpowers. Steele's papers, on the contrary, are little better than trash: there is scarce a thought or sentiment that is worthy to be transferred into a common-place book. My pupil reads a few papers daily, without a single observation on my part. After some time, I remark to him the difference of composition; which, in the course of reading becomes more and more apparent. The last step is to put him on distinguishing the two authors. He at first makes an aukward figure; but I know from trial, that he may be brought to distinguish so readily as sometimes to name the author from the very first period. "Foh! says "he, that is Steele, we'll have no more "of him."

5*th*, DURING infancy, authority should be absolute without relaxation. But let the parents

parents or governor watch the first dawn of reason, which ought to be laid hold of for giving exercise to the judgment of their pupil. They may begin with presenting two simple things, and bidding him chuse for himself. Let them proceed slowly to things less simple. After some exercise of this kind, it is time to demand a reason for his choice. If he be at a loss, a reason may be suggested so slyly, as to make him think it his own, which will raise a desire to find out reasons. Exercise is not more salutary to the body than to the mind. When he wants to have any thing done, let him first try what he can do himself. A savage, having none to apply to for advice or direction, is reduced to judge for himself at every turn: he makes not a single step without thinking before hand what is to follow; by which means, a young savage is commonly endued with more penetration, than an Oxford or Cambridge scholar.

lar. In point of education, I hold it better for a young man to err sometimes on his own judgment, than to follow implicitly the more mature judgment of his preceptor. A boy who is never permitted to think for himself till he is fifteen, will probably continue a boy for life.

HITHERTO of improving our active virtues. We proceed to the improvement of our restraining virtues. When children are very young, the parent has no way for checking an irregular appetite, but authority alone, and this is handled in the section immediately foregoing. When the faculty of reason begins to appear, then is the time for reasoning with your children, and for displaying to them the bad consequences of indulging any irregular appetite. Let them be indulged freely in every thing that tends to their good; but give no quarter to what may

harm

harm them. A young man, accuſtomed from childhood to weigh his inclinations, and to reſtrain ſuch as may prove hurtful, is fitted for making an amiable figure. A young man, on the contrary, who has been gratified in every defire without reſtraint, can never make a good figure. Every ſplendid object ſtrikes his fancy, and raiſes a defire of making it his own. If admitted to a palace, he is mortified that his father's houſe is ſo mean; and ſtill more, that he himſelf makes no figure compared with the landlord. If he meet with a youth more gaily dreſſed than himſelf, he murmurs at the avarice of his parents. Nor can ſuch mortification have an end; for among the numberleſs objects of his wiſhes, there are perhaps very few within his reach. And now to particulars.

1ſt, WHEN any irregular appetite breaks out, endeavour immediately to repreſs it.
Vanity

Vanity, like several other passions, disappoints its aim. Its aim is to make a figure; and yet it renders the person an object of ridicule, never of respect: not to mention, that it lays open an unguarded heart to the machinations of persons ill inclined. Cimon the Athenian amassed a great fortune; but bestowed it liberally on the poor, and on keeping an open table for every person who wanted a dinner. " What comparison, says Plutarch, " between the table of Cimon, simple, " frugal, popular, and that of Lucullus, " contrived for ostentation, and to foster " luxury." Nothing fosters vanity in a young creature so much as dressing it out gorgeously; and yet a fond parent instead of endeavouring to correct that vice, is prone to give it encouragement. When little miss is dressed in her new gown, one would imagine the mother wants to swell its vanity. *Her darling, her little angel*, are appellations liberally bestowed. A child,

perceiving

perceiving this bias in its mother, values dress highly, and despises every one who goes more plain. Is there no hazard that persons thus educated, may come to regard dress as the chief qualification of people of fashion? To correct or restrain an appetite for fine cloaths, the following method among others promises success. Load your girl with ornaments. Say to those in company, that she never looked worse. One adds, is she not pretty enough to become a more simple dress? Take away every superfluous ornament, and then commend her appearance: "How genteel and how sweet she now "looks." The girl will acquire a taste for simplicity. Get your son a coat daubed over with gold or silver, but so ill made as to pain him. Bespeak persons to ridicule him for his finery. He will be glad to change this nasty coat for one more easy and more agreeable. Were it the fashion among people of rank to dress their

their children plain, it would have a wonderful good effect, not only on themselves, but on their inferiors. Young people would learn to despise fine cloaths, and to value themselves on good behaviour: neatness and elegance would be the sole aim in dress. As soon as children are susceptible of verbal instruction, let them know that the chief use of cloaths is to keep them warm; and that to be distinguished by their finery, will make them either be envied or ridiculed.

PHARNABASUS, lord lieutenant to the king of Persia, had invited Agesilaus, king of Lacedemon, to treat of peace; and the interview was in the open field. The first appeared in all the pomp and luxury of the Persian court. He was dressed in a purple robe embroidered with gold and silver: the ground was spread with rich carpets, and fine cushions were laid down to sit on. Agesilaus, in a plain dress,

sat

sat down on the grass without any ceremony. The pride of the Persian was confounded; and he appeared little in the eyes of the beholders compared with the Lacedemonian.

A TUTOR to wean his pupil from a fondness for fine cloaths, told him the following story. There was once upon a time, a very good and a very clever boy named Hercules. Beside his prayers and his book, he was taught to run and leap, to ride, wrestle, and cudgel. And though he was able to beat any boy in the parish, he never harmed any of them. He did not matter cold, nor hunger, nor how or where he lay. He went always dressed in a loose coat of the coarsest kind, which he could put on or off at pleasure. For he knew that his dress was no part of himself, and could neither make him better nor worse. When this brave boy came to man's estate, he went about the world

world doing good; helping the weak, feeding the hungry, cloathing the naked, and chaftifing thofe who did wrong to others. All good people loved him, and all naughty people feared him. But oh fad and difmal! a lady made him a prefent of a new coat laced and ruffled in a moft gorgeous manner; fo that poor Hercules looked as fine as you do now. He turned to this fide, and to that fide; and began to think more and better of himfelf, becaufe he had got this fool's coat upon him. He grow fo fond of it, that he could not bear to have it put off. Neither would he venture out in the rain any more; nor box nor wreftle with any one, for fear of fpoiling his fine coat. So that he loft the love and the praifes of every body; and all people fcorned him, and pointed at him for a fool and a coxcomb.

The fable says, that it was the folly of the cock to spurn the diamond, and to wish for a barley-corn. A more sensible lesson may be drawn from this fable, namely, that we should imitate the cock in distinguishing things of use from things merely of show. The diamond, however sparkling in a fine lady's hair, is of no use to a cock.

A YOUNG man disposed to self-conceit, meets with frequent causes of humiliation: the first affront stings him to the heart. Compare this young man with one who puts no value on himself above his merit. The latter is esteemed by all, caressed by many, and gains some real friends. Modesty is indeed one of the most attractive virtues that belongs to man. The Prince of Condé and the Marischal de Turenne, the greatest generals of their time, possessed each of them that virtue in perfection. It is observed,

that

that thofe who heard them talk of their wars, were furprifed at their referve,— not a word that had the leaft appearance of vanity: they fcarce ever mentioned themfelves. How different the vanity of Cicero, eternally founding his own praifes. Vanity is one of the unlucky paffions that labours againft itfelf: inftead of raifing the man, it leffens him in the efteem of others.

2*d*, MODERATE felf-efteem ought to be cherifhed even in children; and it fprings early, making them afhamed when told that what they have done is below them. Pride is felf-efteem in excefs; which is hateful, and ought to be repreffed by every poffible mortification. Inculcate into your pupil as foon as he is capable of underftanding you, that however diftinguifhed the high may be from the low, the rich from the poor, yet that every one ought to be treated with civility, not excepting

excepting even your servants who depend on you for bread. Paint to him in lively colours the aversion that all have against proud persons; that they can have no friends nor even wellwishers; and therefore, that if he be infected with that disease, he ought carefully to conceal it. Observe to him, that the moderate man is happy, because he is contented with his lot; but that the proud man must be unhappy, because he never thinks himself sufficiently respected.

3*d*, OBSTINACY is a disagreeable quality in society. As in a state, authority and command are confined to a few individuals among multitudes who are tied to obedience, your children ought to be so disciplined, as to yield readily even to those of their own age. Make them sensible, that they will be more praised in yielding, even when they are in the right, than to be stiff and obstinate. Introduce your

your children after their own dinner, to your guests when the desert is on the table. " You shall have, says the mo- " ther, what single thing you chuse, but " nothing unless you all agree." Each will readily renounce what pleases their own palate, rather than get nothing. But to whatever praise a yielding temper may be entitled, instruct your pupil, that it is still more praise-worthy to be obstinate against what is faulty. Too great faci- lity, such as is apt to lead a young per- son astray, is a weakness that ought to be carefully guarded against. Young men are misled, by the vicious inclinations of others, more frequently than by their own: they are ashamed of scrupling to do what their companions do without scruple. Rousseau mentions a young of- ficer, who was averse to the debauche- ries of his fellows; but was carried along from the dread of ridicule. " I am, says " he, like a man who begins to use to-
" bacco :

" bacco: the relish will come by prac-
" tice; and I must not always be a
" child."

4*th*, CURIOSITY about future events is a weakness no less common than hurtful. As human nature is more susceptible of pain than of pleasure, joy from the foresight of good, would be greatly overbalanced by affliction from the foresight of bad. Why then impatiently seek to cross the will of the Deity, who, with watchful benevolence, has hid futurity from us in utter darkness? Banish from the mind of your pupil, prognostics, omens, and such trash, generated by superstition, which harass men more than war or pestilence. Do you wish to know what will befal you? Consult your own principles of action, your condition of life, and the circumstances you are in: these, with experience, will give you all the foresight of futurity that nature intends, or that will be for your good. At any rate, expose not yourself to be laughed at for giving faith to an impostor, who, grossly ignorant of the present, pretends to see into futurity; and who knows as little of your destiny as you do of his *.

5*th*, It

---

* A miserable victim of this delusion was Henry IV. of France, one of the ablest men that ever drew breath. A prediction of some foolish astrologer that he would be murdered, so particular as to name the day, sunk deep into his heart. As the day approached, his mind was in a manner unhinged: he could not eat, sleep, nor rest in a place. The Duc de Sully, who seems to have been no less affected than his master, mentions one circumstance not a little singular, that upon the fatal day he used no precaution for his safety; that, on the contrary, having called for his coach, he forbade the guards to follow him. This famous prediction, which at the time astonished all Europe, would not at present be regarded. Of a hundred such predictions, the ninety-nine that miscarry are instantly forgotten; whereas the single one that happens accidentally to be verified, makes a figure in the imagination, and is recorded as a wonder.

5th, It is a conceit of Aristotle, that every virtue is placed between two opposite vices; which indeed holds in some virtues. Œconomy stands in the middle between avarice and prodigality. Avarice seldom appears in youth: there are however instances of it even in childhood. To check that low appetite, exercise your child in giving away what he is fond of; and caress him if he do it with a good grace. Observe to him, when he can understand you, that avarice is a sneaking vice, below a gentleman; and that it makes a man unhappy, because it makes him grudge to lay out money even on necessaries. Add, that riches are subject to the accidents of fortune; and that an avaricious man, after hoarding up money by starving, may in an instant be deprived of all[*]. On the other hand, as examples make a deeper impression than dry precepts, the best way of extinguishing

[*] See the *Art of Thinking*, No. 27.

guishing any seeds of dissipation in your pupil, is to point out to him men reduced by extravagance from opulence to beggary. If you find him inclined to loose women, carry him to an hospital infected with the most loathsome of all diseases.

6th, The passion that is the most difficult to be restrained, and yet of all the most necessary to be restrained, is anger; which alone has occasioned more mischief than all the other passions together. Experience of its sad consequences may, in a thinking person, do much; and the tutor's lectures, with proper instances, may produce some effect. But there is a simple lesson more easily understood by a young person, and more effectual, which is, to be obstinately silent while he is angry. Let it be kept in memory what Socrates said to a slave who had misbehaved, " I
" would treat thee as thou deservest,
" were

"were I not in a passion." This restraint may be at first difficult; but by due attention in the tutor it will become easy, and prevent every bad effect of the passion. If it be thought too difficult to insist upon so perfect a cure at once, begin with instructing your pupil to copy a Roman Emperor, who made it a rule, that before opening his mouth in wrath, he should repeat leisurely all the letters of the alphabet. I predict such an effect to this simple rule, as in time to lead the pupil to keep silence while any degree of the passion remains. Above all, he should be doubly on his guard when injured or affronted. A fiery temper breaking out upon every insult, is ill qualified for society; if not early restrained, it will occasion manifold distresses. The very best way to avoid great injuries, is to overlook or dissemble what are small. This holds in an especial manner with respect to the female sex. Women, who are not framed for single combat, ought above all things to dread the making a noise in the world. For subduing the impatience of your pupil under an injury, one good method is, to give him examples of distresses occasioned by such impatience. In the history of ancient Greece, there is a glorious instance of the good effects of restraint. Euribiades, admiral of the Grecian fleet collected against the Persians, angry to be opposed in the council of war by Themistocles a young officer, brandished his staff in a threatening manner. " Strike, " said Themistocles, but hear me first." Subdued by this signal instance of self-command, Euribiades listened, followed the advice of the young officer, and obtained a complete victory. The cool behaviour of Themistocles saved Greece, which probably would have been ruined by the old general. Pericles the Athenian general, was attacked one day in the public forum, before the people, by a brutish

brutish fellow, with much opprobrious language. And in his return home, he was followed by the same person, venting his wrath in the same stile. It being now dark, he ordered his servant to light the man home, for fear he should lose his way. Arcadius an Argive, who had been in a course of reviling Philip king of Macedon, was apprehended and brought before him; but was courteously treated, and sent away with presents. The king being informed that the Argive had changed his note, and was full of his praises, " Look you now, says he, am not I a " better physician than any of you? I " have cured a foul mouth'd fellow by " presents, which would not have been " done had I followed your advice of " punishing him."

The *third* head contains a few relative matters, to which we proceed.

1*st*, For

1*st*, For training young people to bear disappointments, facts may contribute as well as precepts. Give your children hopes of what will be agreeable, a ball for example, a race, the return of a brother after a long absence; and upon the disappointment, exhort them to bear it with a good grace: this will have a much finer effect than exhortations in general. But let the disappointment appear to proceed from chance; for if they perceive your intention, they will conclude that it was done to vex them, not to improve their temper. A gentleman, though otherways of good understanding, erred in this branch of education. He had three comely girls between twelve and sixteen; and to enure them to bear disappointments, he would propose to make a visit, which he knew would delight them. The coach was ordered; and the young ladies, completely armed for conquest, were ready to take their seats. But behold!

behold! their father had changed his mind. This indeed was a disappointment; but as it appeared to proceed from whim or caprice, it might four their temper instead of improving it. Children are early sensible of ill treatment; and when the parental authority is too far stretched, a child obeys from fear, not from affection.

2*d*, It is a capital duty in parents, to teach their children to bear with and excuse the faults of their companions. There are even adult persons who perceive no blemish in one they love, nor any virtue in one they hate. To correct that wrong bias in young persons, is not an easy undertaking, nor to be attempted till they have acquired some share of understanding. Talk to your pupils of their companions. Point out faults, which however are so slight, compared with their good qualities, as to make them not the less deserving of affection. Instruct your pupils, that perfection is not to be found in any human being: bid them reflect whether they themselves are entirely exempt from failings. And conclude with observing, that among friends and companions, it is a sweet commerce to forgive one another. If proper opportunities be taken, such lessons will produce two good effects, namely, to excuse the faults of a friend, and to respect virtue in an enemy: the latter will soften enmity; and the former will cement friendship.

3*d*, In the third section, at the beginning, are contained instructions for keeping children always employed. I here add several particulars on the same subject, fitted for children farther advanced in years. A girl of eight or nine, may be trained to assist her mother in serving the guests at table. Let her be seated within

in reach of a pudding, or of any thing that requires little carving, ready to help thofe who call for it. In a fhort time, fhe may be employed in diffecting a chicken, or even a pullet. The notion of being ufeful, and behaving like her mamma, infpires her with a certain dignity of behaviour, and fets her above childifh amufements. It has pained me to fee a young woman of feventeen or eighteen, applying a knife fo aukwardly, as with difficulty to diffect what is on her own plate. How mean muft be her appearance at the head of her own table! I am acquainted with the miftrefs of a great family, who gives ftill more employment to her daughter, not above the age of feven. The child is directed to infpect the bed-rooms, that every thing may be in order for the guefts. A company were to depart about eight in the morning. " Child," fays the lady, " I " perhaps may not be up fo early. Be
" ready

"ready to attend the company: see that every thing be prepared for breakfast; and be sure to attend them to their coach."

4th, NEXT of an article that ought not to be neglected, and yet is not a little difficult, which is to accustom children to acknowledge their faults. It is not sufficient that parents, by gentle treatment, have acquired the affection of their children: education will go on but imperfectly, if children be not also trained to place confidence in their parents, and to apply to them freely in every difficulty. The nicest point of all, is to enure them to an ingenuous confession of faults, the only case in which I approve auricular confession. This practice, early commenced, will soon become habitual. A child cuts a finger, or breaks a china cup. It is unhappy till it acquaint its father or mother how it happened. Let a candid

did acknowledgment be an abfolute pardon: let it be the part of the parent to mitigate the fault; and to obferve, that the child deferves more praife for its frank confeffion, than blame for the fault it has committed; that the fear of difcovery when a fault is concealed, makes a heavy heart; but that the heart is relieved by a fair confeffion. Affection to parents leads children to put confidence in them. What is there to obftruct that confidence, but harfhnefs and feverity? A child will never confefs a fault, if afraid to be ill treated: it will diffemble, it will lie, it will do any thing to avoid difcovery. When a child withdraws from its parents and makes any other perfon its confident, farewel to education. But when children are treated kindly, they never think of any confident but the perfon who takes care of them. By kindly treatment, the heart is laid open, and every wrong bias is difcovered, which afford a fair opportunity for good culture. Let us look forward to a child's riper years, and reflect on a habit of candour and ingenuity thus acquired: what anxious thoughts, what diffimulation, muft this charming habit have prevented!

Among the various ways of training children to confefs their faults, the following can fcarce fail of being fuccefsful. Returning home after a vifit of a week or two, put each of your children to fay, what good has been done by the reft; and what ill itfelf has done. The former endears them to one another, the latter reftrains them from committing faults. Make thefe articles the fubject of converfation: endeavour to ripen the underftanding of the young creatures, by fhowing them what is right and what is wrong. But be careful to provide a trufty perfon to inform you of any fault that has been concealed. Say to the child flightly, " Surely

"Surely, my dear, you have a bad memory, did you not do so and so." It will think it vain to hide, as " Papa or Mamma knows every thing."

It is a pregnant sign of a good disposition, that a child of itself corrects a fault. A girl between three and four, having got a present of fruit, was desired by its mother to give part of it to her companions. Having reserved a large share to herself, she distributed the rest, giving some to an elder sister, now a woman. After devouring what she had retained, she desired back her sister's share, and got it. The mother expostulated, but in vain; and having left the room, the sister said, "My dear, I make you welcome to the fruit, but you behave ill in disobeying your mamma." This gentle reproof, having touched the child in the tender part, that of obedience, had its effect. After a day or two, she requested more

fruit

fruit from her mother, which, with an air of satisfaction she carried to the sister. Correction may be necessary sometimes; but for a child to correct a fault of its own accord, is extremely pleasant. A child about three years of age, took some cotton thread which Miss B— was sowing upon muslin. " Pray child give me " the cotton, you will dirty it." The child refusing, Miss B—, laying aside her work, said gravely, " Would you have " been pleased had I dirtied your doll?" Some weeks after, the child observing cotton thread in the hands of another young lady, begged earnestly for it to give to Miss B—. Such instances suggest the following rule. When a child from petulence or perverseness misbehaves grossly, stern authority ought to be interposed. In other faults, expostulation and advice are far better.

A VOLUNTARY confeſſion is a ſtill more pregnant ſign of a good diſpoſition. A young lady aged eleven, of a rank higher than which there are none, having hurt a finger accidentally, ſhowed ſome degree of impatience. The governeſs, having in vain endeavoured to ſhame her out of it, left the room with a reproachful look, ſaying, that ſhe could not bear to ſee ſuch concern for a mere trifle. In leſs than an hour, ſhe received a billet from her pupil, acknowledging her miſbehaviour, and intreating to be forgiven. Happy temper! the richeſt gift that nature has to beſtow, and of which nature is far from being prodigal. Few there are of any rank who are bleſſed with a temper ſo pliant; fewer ſtill of high rank. But the praiſe muſt not be attributed entirely to temper: ſeldom is pure nature ſo refined. The young lady owes much to an affectionate mother, whoſe high ſtation has not made her relax from the e-ducation

ducation of her children, with a degree of prudence and fagacity, that would give luftre to perfons much inferior in rank.

5*th*, CHILDREN are far from being all of them equally flexible. It required a week to make a boy of two years dip his fingers in water after dinner. Example had no effect, nor exhortation. The mother put into the glafs fruit he was fond of: neither did that prevail. She thought at laft of the gardener's fon, a child of the fame age, who readily dipt his fingers and laid hold of the fruit. Emulation prevailed: young mafter dipped his fingers inftantly. I am pleafed with the ingenuity of the mother; but relifh not the ftruggling againft accidental averfions, which time will correct without trouble. Authority, inftead of fubduing, tends to rivet fuch an averfion. It is not always eafy to diftinguifh an acquired averfion

from

from what is natural; and when authority is interpofed, may not there be a hazard of ftruggling againft nature? Many furely will remember certain eatables abhorred by them when children, which at prefent they are fond of without having fuffered perfecution. In health, nature is the fureft guide in the choice of food. The fame food may be falutary at one period of life, and not at another. Will parents pretend to be wifer than nature? I am far, however, from wifhing to have children indulged in whim or fancy. If a child refufe what is fet before it, hunger will foon bring it to order. If it conftantly refufe after repeated trials, the averfion muft have a deeper root than whim or fancy.

Many perfons fpeak well and with propriety, but how few are there who liften patiently and properly to what is urged againft their opinion? It has accordingly

cordingly been obferved, that it is no lefs difficult to produce a habit of hearing with attention, than of expreffing well what deferves to be heard. Yet, early example and good inftruction, will do much to train young perfons to a more agreeable manner of converfation.

SECT.

SECT. V.

INSTRUCTIONS *that occasionally may be applied in every Stage of Education.*

1*st*, NEGLECT no favourable opportunity of instilling into your pupils, that a man ought to be regarded in proportion to the good he does; and that compared with the being useful, the distinction between rich and poor, high and low, ought to be of little estimation; that an industrious peasant who educates his children to be useful members of society, is entitled to more respect than the great lord, who, in the midst of indigent neighbours, lavishes immense sums upon himself, without ever thinking of others.

2*d*, MAKE your pupil sensible, that in order to save for charity or benevolence, œconomy is an estimable virtue. Augustus Cæsar, Emperor of Rome, never wore

wore a garment but what was spun by his wife Livia or his sister Octavia. Scipio, the glory of Rome and terror of Carthage, dressed his garden with his own hands. The venerable old senator Fabricius, illustrious by many triumphs, supped commonly on the herbs that he himself had raised. A stranger who wishes to be well received, ought to be handsomely dressed; but a plain coat fits better on a man of known eminence, who will be copied by others, without derogating from his rank.

3*d*, SELF-LOVE makes us labour for ourselves; benevolence makes us labour for others: emulation is added to enforce these motives to action. Emulation, inherent in the nature of man, appears even in children: they strive for victory without knowing what makes them strive. Emulation kept within proper bounds is an useful principle, and

and far from being unsociable: it becomes only so, when by excess it degenerates into envy. Why then is it banished by Rousseau, from his system of education? Was it his purpose to distinguish his *Eleve* from the rest of mankind, by a peculiar nature? Approbation is bestowed on those who behave well; but in struggling for victory, the hope of being approved is a very faint motive compared with emulation. Through the force of that incitement, a young man will persevere in acquiring knowledge, who without it, would have made no progress. It ought, therefore, to be the study of every teacher, to give such a direction to emulation in his pupil, as to produce the greatest effect. A crowd of competitors damps it: a very small number is not sufficient to rouse it. The proper stage for emulation, is a private school, admitting not above twelve or fifteen disciples.

ciples. A family of six or seven children, may give exercise to it.

4*th*, WITH respect to the improvement of memory, it is severe to make children get by heart prayers, psalms, or other dry compositions, which they neither relish, nor can well understand. Put into their hands short historical ballads that make virtuous impressions, or give lively descriptions of objects they are acquainted with, especially of the gay and ludicrous kind. These they will get by heart of their own accord, and be fond to repeat them to their parents or their companions. This exercise ought to be entirely voluntary. Were the getting a thing by heart imposed as a task, it would be easy to some and a heavy burden upon others. Emulation ought to be here excluded, except, perhaps, among boys who are found to be equal in point of memory.

5*th*, FRAUD

5th, FRAUD or deceit ought to be carefully watched; and even the flighteft appearances ought to be condignly punifhed. I had the following ftory from a lady who was an eye-witnefs. Tom and Will were two fine boys; the eldeft about eight, fenfible, infinuating, and fo acute as to comprehend even the moral of many fables of Æfop. Will, a year younger, was a mild, tractable boy. One day having got fome halfpence, Tom purchafed a peacock of gingerbread, Will a horfe of the fame ftuff, both fhining with gold. The moifture of Tom's little hand grafping his treafure eagerly, and a little nibbling to tafte its fweets, had, by the time they got home, entirely defaced the peacock, while the horfe, delighting Will's eye more than his palate, was perfectly entire. Tom coveting now his brother's horfe, propofed an exchange, and by deceit and artifice prevailed. This tranfaction reached the mother. She
called

called the boys before her, heard evidence, and pronounced the following sentence. " Will, seeing you have made " the exchange willingly, you have no " remedy though you have been decei- " ved. Take care only that you be not " deceived a second time. As for you " Thomas, you are not to profit by " cheating your brother — throw the " horse into the fire." Tom, whom conscience had made a coward, was hedging away, lucky to escape so easily; but was stopped by the judge. "Come back young " man, bring your Æsop's fables, and " point out to me the fable that re- " sembles your case." The spectators muttered, " better whip him at once than " engage him in an attempt above his " comprehension." But the mother was not mistaken in her son. He turned every leaf over, and with affected ignorance, asked if it was the ass and the lap dog. No. Will it be the cock on the dunghill?

dunghill? No. May be it is the fox in the carver's shop. "No sir, you know "well it is none of these; but don't put "off your time and mine, the longer you "trifle, the more severe will be your pu- "nishment." The boy seeing it vain to parry, presented with a burst of tears, the picture of the thief biting off his mother's ear. "You see, said the judge, "what a bad mother I should be, if I "left your crime unpunished." She retired with the criminal, and did not spare the rod. This probably was the first transgression of the kind; and who knows what might have followed, had it been indulged or passed as a joke. Thomas is now in the service of the public; and his Majesty has not a more sensible, upright servant.

6*th*, THERE is no branch of discipline that ought to be exercised with more caution, than the distribution of rewards and punishments. If money, a fine coat, or what pleases the palate, be the reward promised; is it not the ready way to foment avarice, vanity, or luxury? Praise is an efficacious reward, of which even children are fond; and when properly applied, it never fails to produce good behaviour. Punishment requires still more caution; as it ought to be proportioned to the temper of the pupil, as well as to the nature of the fault. Obstinacy which is inherent in some persons, may sometimes require corporal punishment. Lying I think may be corrected, or rather prevented, by proper management: my reason is, that it is not inherent in our nature, but forced upon a child by harsh treatment. Most faults that a child can be guilty of, may be repressed by shame and disgrace, which sink deep into the heart of children, as well as of adult persons. To keep children in awe by the fear of corporal punishment, will put them

upon

upon hiding their faults, inftead of correcting them *.

I GLADLY lay hold of this opportunity to make a general obfervation, of no flight importance with refpect to education. Among favages, whofe ruling paffions are anger and refentment, authority is fupported by no other means but force and fear. That rude practice prevails even among polifhed nations. Schools for education were erected upon the principle of punifhment; very unhappily indeed, as punifhment, inftead of foftening or improving manners, tends to harden thofe who fuffer by it. Humanity in time prevailed over vicious education; and a facred truth was difcovered, that man is a creature from whom every thing may be obtained by love, nothing by fear. The feverity of fchool-punifhments has

* Si cui tam eft mens illiberalis, ut objurgatione non corrigatur: is etiam ad plagas, ut peffima quæque mancipia, durabitur. *Quintil.* lib. 1. c. 3.

has gradually yielded to the conviction of this important truth; and yet such is the force of custom, that instances remain, not a few, of the old stile of education. To dwell upon these instances, would be irksome: I confine myself to one, illustrious indeed, as it relates to Eton, a school in high vogue. In that school there stands, exposed to open view, the terrible block that the boys must kneel upon to receive a flogging, perhaps as often from the bad humour of the master, as from the demerit of the sufferer. And that the boys may never lose sight of punishment, matters are so contrived, as to furnish examples once a week at least, chiefly on Monday, which in the language of the school, has obtained the illustrious appellation of the day of doom. Would one imagine, that a discipline so brutal, should stand firm, even against the humanity of our present manners? Glad am I to be able to

give

give testimony in favour of my native country, that in our schools, few traces remain of that inhuman practice. I dare not say none, were I even to keep within the capital.

7*th*, THE difference between the being serious and jocular is taught by nature, and it is comprehended even by infants. But the telling stories in jest ought not to be early practised on children. Truth and sincerity cannot be too early inculcated; nor, till these are firmly established, ought such jests to be attempted. Let the first essays be plain and obvious, so as to prevent the possibility of a mistake in the pupil. More disguise may in time be used, according to his capacity; but always so as to afford no room for a mistake. It is indeed a useful branch of education, that persons intended for society should understand a joke; but let the practice be never so far indulged as to to impinge, in any degree, on the sacred authority of truth. When young persons come to understand the difference between jest and earnest in those they converse with, the next step in point of discipline, is to inure them to bear a joke with temper. Practice is necessary; and the only way is to begin with slight jokes, and to go on at intervals till they can bear what are more cutting. The first trials should always be when your pupil is in good humour; nor should a severe joke ever be attempted, but when he is in very good humour.

8*th*, OF all that children can be taught, I am acquainted with no lesson of greater importance, than to be satisfied with the station we are placed in by Providence. This lesson comes in properly here; because, by various ways, it may be inculcated in every stage of education. The following fable may make an impression, even in the first or second stage. In a beautiful river there lived three silver trouts. Though they wanted for nothing, two of them grew sad and discontented; taking no pleasure in what they enjoyed, but always longing for something better. To punish their discontent it was intimated to them by their maker, that they should have whatever they wished for. Give me, says the eldest, wings like the birds of the air; and then I shall be happy. At first he had great pleasure in flying. He mounted high, and looked down with scorn on all the fishes in the world. He flew over rivers and mountains, till, growing faint with hunger, he came to the ground for some refreshment. He happened to alight among dry sands and rocks, where there was nothing either to eat or drink. And thus he ended his days in great misery.

The second trout said, I do not wish for wings to ramble into strange places, where I do not know what may become of me. I should be contented and happy, were I instructed to avoid the snares of men and other dangers. His mind being enlightened, he said to himself, I shall now be the happiest of fishes. He took great care to keep out of harm's way. When he saw a fly skimming on the water, or a worm carried down the stream, he durst not bite for fear of a hook. Thus he kept himself in a continual alarm, and durst neither eat nor sleep for fear of mischief. He pined away; and at last died for fear of dying, the most miserable of all deaths.

The youngest trout said, that he was satisfied with his lot; and that he had no wish but to be always content, and to be resigned to the will of his maker. Thus, this little trout slept always in peace, and
wakened

wakened in gladness: whatever happened, he was still pleased and thankful. In a word, he was the happiest of all fishes; because content and resignation to the will of our maker are the chief ingredients of happiness.

WHAT follows is more proper for the last stage. Direct the attention of your pupil to chearful objects, and train him to look on their contraries as shades in a picture, which add force to the luminous parts, and beauty to the whole. Accustom him to see every thing in the most favourable light; to behold the luxury of the times as giving food to the hungry and cloathing to the naked; to look upon the horrors of war as productive of the blessings of peace; and upon the miseries of many with a thankful heart, that his own lot has been more favourable.

9th, The laſt recommendation I ſhall give on the preſent head, is, that young perſons, male and female, ſhould have always at hand a common-place book, for keeping in remembrance obſervations made in reading, reflecting, converſing, travelling. The advantages are manifold. *Firſt*, It keeps the attention awake, in order that nothing of importance may eſcape. Conſider this practice as to reading. A perſon who reads merely for amuſement, gives little attention: ideas glide through the mind, and vaniſh inſtantly. But let a common-place book be in view: attention is on the ſtretch to find matter, and impreſſions are made that the memory retains. *Next*, The judgment is in conſtant exerciſe, in order to diſtinguiſh what particulars deſerve remembrance. *Third*, Perſeverance in this practice, brings on a habit of expreſſing our thoughts readily and diſtinctly. *Fourth*, A facility of writing currently is acquired.

acquired. And, in the *laſt* place, it fills up time pleaſantly, and makes activity habitual.

10*th*, THE following hints reſpect more immediately the conduct of parents and tutors. The bad habits that children are apt to acquire from ſervants, are an obſtruction to education. I know of no remedy, but to keep children as much as poſſible under the eye of their parents. This will be no reſtraint, if they be fond of their parents; which they always are, when kindly treated and indulged in innocent freedom. It ſhould be held as a puniſhment for a fault, to be ordered down ſtairs among the ſervants. But this requires circumſpect conduct on the part of the parents; for they muſt carefully avoid the doing or ſaying of any thing but what they wiſh their children to imitate. It is amazing, how early children adopt the manners of thoſe they

are

are among. This circumspection ought to be extended even to the persons who are hired to attend them.

Let truth prevail in all your instructions: in reasoning with your children, never use any artifice. Some children are quick of discernment: the discovery of an artifice will tempt them to pay their guides in the same coin.

The keeper ought to be well acquainted with the mute language of the infant under her care. An infant cries from bodily pain. It cries when it is hungry; and gives over when it sees things prepared for feeding it. It is not uncommon in a child at play, to fall a-crying; not from anger, but from inability to express what it wants. If the keeper be ignorant of what troubles the child, she will be at a loss about a remedy.

If a child have any defect in its shape that cannot easily be hid, let the defect be frankly acknowledged, and even made a joke of at times. This will prevent whispering, which always makes a defect appear worse than it really is. Philopemen, the greatest General of his age, was of a mean appearance. He went to an invited dinner in his camp-dress, without a single attendant. Being taken for one of the General's servants, he was ordered to the kitchen to cut logs for the fire. His friend the landlord, seeing him in his waistcoat at that work, " Bless me " General," says he, " what are you do- " ing here? I am," answers the General, " paying for my bad looks."

SECT. VI.

PECULIARITIES *respecting the Education of* FEMALES.

1st, THE different instincts of the two sexes appear very early. A boy is continually in action, loves a drum, a top, or riding on a stick. A girl, wishing to be agreeable, is fond of ornaments that please the eye. She begins with a doll, which she dresses and undresses, to try what ornaments will suit best. In due time, the doll is laid aside; and the young woman's own person becomes the object of her attention. This instinct rightly directed, advances from propriety of dress to that of behaviour, still in order to please. Employ therefore a young girl upon what will adorn her: she will apply to the needle more willingly than to reading or writing. As she advances, let her be taught the art of drawing, not human figures, which cannot be made ornamental, but leaves, flowers, and such things as tend to enliven her dress. Children are fond of lively colours; and hence their taste for showy dress and ornaments of gold and silver. Here the prudent mother interposes with a lesson, " that " dress ought to be suited to the age and " rank of the wearer; that simplicity is " becoming in dress as well as in man- " ners; that the fashion should not be " totally disregarded, but that it ought to " yield to propriety." A fond mother never thinks of such a lesson; beauty is exalted above every qualification: and if a girl have any share of it, dress alone is studied. If to her looks can be added a genteel air and elegant motion in dancing or walking, she becomes a perfect angel. Thus, external appearance is highly cultivated, and little attention given either to the head or heart. Is it wonderful, that

that a young woman so educated, should make but an aukward figure in educating her own children?

Females have a flexible tongue, and acquire more early than males the use of speech: their voice is sweeter; and they talk more. A man says what he knows; a woman, what is agreeable: knowledge is necessary to the former; taste is sufficient to the latter. The politeness of men consists in offering service; of women, in making themselves agreeable. In the politeness of men, there is more or less of dissimulation; none in that of women, for they love to be agreeable. Hence it is, that politeness has a more pleasing air in young women, than in young men.

2*d*, A man's conduct depends mostly on the approbation of his own conscience; that of a woman, greatly on the opinion of others. A man who does his duty, can brave censure: a woman's conduct ought to be exemplary, in order to be esteemed by all. The least doubt of her chastity, deprives her of every comfort in the matrimonial state. In the education of females accordingly, no motive has a greater influence, than the thought of what people will say of them. Boys are not so tractable: it requires much discipline to make them bend to the opinion of others. Hence, to be esteemed by all, modesty and reserve are essential in young women; to acquire which, they ought to be taught early to suppress their desires, and to have a strict attention to decency and decorum. But under such restraint, let the occupations of young women be made as agreeable as possible. A girl who loves her mother or her governess, will work the whole day at her side without wearying, provided she be allowed to prattle, which is her favourite

favourite amufement. A girl who loves not her mother above all the world, feldom turns to good. Even confinement properly managed, rivets her attachment; becaufe children are made fenfible by nature, that obedience is their duty, and that it is good for them to be governed. Indulge gaiety, indulge laughter, indulge play, but ftill within moderate bounds. Draw them frequently from play to work, but in fo foft a way as to prevent murmuring: cuftom will make the change eafy, and produce in time entire fubmiffion to the mother's will. This is effential to the female fex, for ever fubjected to the authority of a fingle perfon, or to the opinion of all.

3*d*, FEMALE children ought to be hardily bred, not only for their own health, but to have a healthy offspring. Chiefly with a view to the latter, it was fafhionable for the Spartan young ladies to mix with

with the men in military games, not excepting wreſtling and other violent exerciſes. This ſurely was not prompted by nature, which does not intend women to be ſo robuſt. For the ſake of health, all that is neceſſary, is plain food, with frequent walking or riding.

4*th*, At Athens, the young women appeared frequently in public, but ſeparate from the young men. In every feaſt, in every ſacrifice, in every public ſolemnity, the daughters of the principal citizens were introduced, crowned with flowers, dancing in parties, ſinging hymns, and preſenting offerings to their deities. Such exerciſes, beſide contributing to health, formed the taſte of the young women to what is proper and agreeable; and made them objects of deſire without hazarding their morals. In France, the education of young women is very different. They are ſhut up in a convent, and never taſte freedom

freedom till they are married. A fystem of education more subversive of morals, is scarce within the reach of invention. Unnatural confinement in a convent, makes a young woman embrace with avidity every pleasure, when she is set free. To relish domestic life, one must be acquainted with it; for it is in the house of her parents that a young woman acquires the relish. A discreet matron will attend her daughters to an assembly, to an opera, to the play-house; but she will instruct them, that the pleasure they find there, ought to be considered as an amusement merely, unfit to employ much of the time of young women, who are destined by nature to govern a family. What can be more preposterous than the behaviour of an idle woman, leading her daughters from riot to riot, without giving admission to a sedate thought? A lady carried to Bath her two daughters, aged between twelve and fourteen, in order

der to give them fome notion of living in public. Their natural gaiety, fhe thought, would be improved by the gaiety of the place; that the company at Bath would contribute to form their manners; and that they were too young to fuffer from their male companions. It was her opinion, that her daughters were of a proper age for relifhing public meetings, without lofing the tafte of domeftic tranquillity.

5*th*, In training young women, exhibit every thing to them in an agreeable light; and in particular, fuffer them not to imagine that there can be any pain in doing what is right. Is it painful for a young woman to make herfelf amiable in order to be loved, to make herfelf eftimable in order to be efteemed, to behave honourably in order to be honoured? The influence of a young woman, commences with her virtues. What

man

man is there, however rough in temper, who foftens not his behaviour to a young woman of fixteen, interefting even by her bafhfulnefs, and commanding that refpect from all which fhe beftows on all? Virtue is effential to genuine love. To fupport that fweet paffion in any refined degree, there muft be mutual efteem, which cannot fubfift without virtue. How defpicable in my eyes muft that creature be, with whom I have no connection but for the fake merely of animal defire?

APPENDIX to SECTION VI.

AFTER fo much dry matter, fome relaxation will probably be made welcome; and in that view the following female characters are prefented. The firft, by Marivaux, is a character of which benignity of heart is the ruling principle.

MADAME

MADAME de Miran had confiderable remains of beauty; but there appeared in her countenance, fomething fo good and fo rational as to obfcure thefe remains. Franknefs and good nature are not friendly to love. We admire the woman, but her graces make little impreffion: we enjoy her company, without thinking that fhe is pretty, but only that fhe is the beft creature in the world. I have accordingly heard little of Madame de Miran's lovers, but much of her friends. It is reported, that fhe had friends even of her own fex; which I can believe, confidering her plain and innocent mien, which gave no jealoufy to her female companions, and made her appear more like a confident than a rival.

To a phyfiognomy more pleafing than bewitching, to eyes demanding amity more than love, was added a genteel figure, which might have given defire had she so inclined; but she never studied any motion but what was necessary.

With respect to her understanding, I know not that any one ever thought of praising it; nor do I know that any one ever said it was deficient. It was of a sort that is listened to attentively; but without being censured or applauded.

Even in matters of indifference, Madame de Miran said nothing, thought nothing, but what verified that abounding goodness which was the foundation of her character. But do not imagine it to be a silly or blind goodness, ridiculed even by those whom it serves. Her's was a virtue, an emanation from an excellent heart, which never exerted itself at the expence of reason, nor of justice. She had not indeed any of that quality termed nobleness of soul: her goodness was more simple, more amiable, though less splendid.

splendid. I have known persons with that same nobleness of soul, who had not the best hearts in the world. They were so occupied with the pleasure of being generous, as to be negligent of being just. Such persons loved to be praised: Madame de Miran never once thought of deserving praise: she never exerted an act of benevolence in order to gratify herself, but in order to relieve you. If you expressed much gratitude to her, what flattered her the most was to find you satisfied.

I HAD almost forgot one thing, not a little singular. Though this lady never vaunted of her own good deeds, you might vaunt to her of yours with all security. The pleasure of hearing you say that you was good, made your vanity pass unobserved, or made her think it excusable.

As to those tiresome creatures who value themselves upon trifles, who are vain of their rank or their riches, they gave no vexation to Madame de Miran: she had no affection for them, and that was all. Babblers who slander others, though without intention, gave offence to the goodness of her nature; whereas the vain offended her reason only. She bore the loquacious with temper; smiling only at the fatigue they gave her, without ever suspecting it. In company with the whimsical or headstrong, who listen not to reason, she had patience, and was nevertheless their friend. "They are ho-"neft people," she observed, "they have "their little failings, and who is without "them?" A coquet who insists upon being admired, was lower in her esteem than a woman who once in her life had been more in love than a woman ought to be; it being less faulty in her opinion to misbehave once, than perpetually to be tempting others to misbehave.

This lady considered religion as chiefly intended to enforce moral duties. She respected those who bestow their whole time on exercises of devotion, but without ever thinking of joining them. Never had any person better reason to be convinced of the benignity of the Deity: her conviction proceeded from her heart; and no person had a better heart. She accordingly loved God sincerely, without being disturbed with any superstitious terrors.

The next portrait is of a lady every way accomplished, done by the same hand.

Madame Dorsin was beautiful; and yet it was not her beauty that even at first made the strongest impression. It yielded to another impression. This wants explanation.

explanation. Perfonify beauty; and fuppofe her uneafy for being fo ftrikingly beautiful; that fhe wifhes to be agreeable only; and that fhe endeavours to leffen her beauty, but without hiding it altogether. Such would be the countenance of Madame Dorfin.

But here I talk only of her looks, what may be expreffed in a portrait. Add a foul that animated her looks, that rendered them as delicate, as lively, as elevated, as ferious, as jocular, as fhe herfelf was by turns; and then you will be able to imagine in her looks, an infinity of expreffions beyond the reach of painting. Let us now examine that foul, fince we are on the fubject. When one has little fpirit, it is commonly attributed to defective organs. An acquaintance, talking on this fubject, faid gravely and in learned terms, " that the foul is more or lefs " confined, more or lefs embarraffed, ac-
" cording

"cording to the organs to which it is "united." If so, nature must have conferred on Madame Dorsin organs in high perfection; for never was a soul more agile than hers, nor less confined in its operations.

THE spirit that most women exert, is acquired, not natural. One expresses herself carelessly and with seeming indifference, to make people believe that she cannot take the trouble of thinking. One talks with a serious and decisive air. One deals in refined thoughts, and pronounces them in a tone that calls for attention. One affects to be lively and loud. Madame Dorsin affected none of these peculiarities. It was the subject that gave a tone to her thoughts; and it was her thoughts that gave a tone to her expression. I hope to be understood when I say, that her spirit had no sex; and that it was enchanting when she was in humour

mour to display it. Few pretty women but are over fond to please; and hence those little affectations which virtually say, *behold me.* Such apeish tricks were not relished by Madame Dorsin: her pride would not admit her to descend so low. If upon any occasion she relaxed a little, no one was sensible of it but herself. In general, she valued her understanding more than her beauty: it was her you honoured in praising the former: it was her figure only, in praising the latter. To appear agreeable was not her study: it would have made her blush if you could say, " That lady has endea-" voured to make me fond of her." In a word, the only coquetry she could be suspected of, was her willingness that you should be sensible, how much she despised all the little arts of pleasing.

From her understanding we proceed to the qualities of her heart. Her goodness
equalled

equalled that of Madame de Miran, but was of a different cast. Goodness in the latter was connected with plain sense: in the former, it was connected with superior understanding, which makes it always show in the most advantageous light. When one confers a favour on me, and seems ignorant of its importance, my pride is not alarmed, a slight return of gratitude is in my opinion sufficient. But a favour done me with a thorough sense of its importance, humbles my pride, and lays on me a heavy burden of gratitude. This was not the only respect in which the goodness of Madame Dorsin differed from that of her friend. People seldom have the courage to display all their wants. Madame de Miran served you chearfully, but literally, seeing no farther. Madame Dorsin, discovering your wants from your imperfect hints, served you to the utmost of your wishes. It was not her you fatigued with your

Z   concerns

concerns: she fatigued you. It was you she advised, pressed, chid for being negligent. She in a word made your affair her own: the interest she took in you appeared so much her own concern, as to lose entirely the character of generosity. Instead of thinking as most people do, " I have served this man, and he " owes me much gratitude," Madame Dorsin's notion was, " I have served this " man frequently, I have accustomed " him to depend on me, I must not dis- " appoint him." Your boldness in demanding a favour charmed her, and was all the gratitude she wished. It was treating her according to her own heart.

It is not easy for people of spirit to bring themselves down to a level with those who have none—they cannot find a subject low enough. Madame Dorsin, though she had a greater share of spirit than

than those who have much, yet never assumed more spirit than others had. She thought that no human being is entitled to laugh at the imperfections of others. Those who had spirit were fond to display it in her presence; not as necessary to please her, but to honour themselves. She indulged her female companions to talk at their ease, seldom interrupting but to approve, to praise, and to allow them to draw breath.

Men differing in rank and condition, seldom make good company together. Each displays what distinguishes him above the rest. In Madame Dorsin's house, there was no thought of rank, nor of any other distinction. They were men who conversed with men; and the strongest reason always prevailed. The superiority of her genius inspired every one.

To an excellent heart, to a diftinguifhed underftanding, was joined a foul fuperior to events; which could be afflicted but not dejected, and which in diftrefs one never thinks of pitying, but of praifing. I have feen her more than once in affliction; but could never obferve, that it had any effect on the fweetnefs of her manners, nor on her tranquillity in converfing with her friends: fhe gave her attention wholly to them, though fhe had caufe to give it wholly to herfelf.

She was adored by her domeftics; who held themfelves rich becaufe fhe was fo, and confidered every misfortune happening to her as happening to themfelves. So little notion had they of a feparate intereft, that in every particular they joined themfelves with her, "We have gain-"ed a caufe, we have purchafed a farm, "we have loft a friend." She was highly generous; but the œconomy of her domeftics domestics made all up. Judge how amiable the mistress must have been, to tame, to enchant, a species of beings, the very best of whom can scarce pardon us for their servitude, or for our superiority.

THE next portrait is drawn by the celebrated Rousseau, exhibiting the character of a young woman virtuously educated.

SOPHIA is not a beauty, but in her presence beauties are discontented with themselves. At first, she scarcely appears pretty; but the more she is beheld, the more agreeable she appears. She gains when others lose, and what she gains she never loses. She is equalled by none in a sweet expression of countenance; and without dazzling beholders, she interests them. She loves dress, and is a good judge of it; despises finery, but dresses with peculiar grace; mixing simplicity
with

with elegance. Ignorant she is of what colours are in fashion; but knows well what suits her complexion. She covers her beauties, but so slightly or rather artfully, as to give play to the imagination. She prepares herself for managing a family of her own, by managing that of her father. Cookery is familiar to her, with the price and quality of provisions; and she is a ready accountant. Her chief view however is to serve her mother and lighten her cares. She holds cleanness and neatness to be indispensable in a woman; and that a slattern is disgusting, especially if beautiful.

The attention given to externals, does not make her overlook her more material duties. Sophia's understanding is solid, without being profound. Her sensibility is too great for a perfect equality of temper; but her sweetness renders that inequality harmless. A harsh word does not

not make her angry; but her heart swells, and she retires to disburden it by weeping. Recalled by her father or mother, she comes at the instant, wiping her eyes and appearing chearful. She suffers with patience any wrong done her; but is impatient to repair any wrong she has done, and does it so cordially as to make it appear meritorious. If she happen to disoblige a companion, her joy and her caresses, when restored to favour, show the burden that lay upon her good heart.

The love of virtue is Sophia's ruling passion. She loves it, because no other thing is so lovely: she loves it, because it is the glory of the female sex: she loves it as the only road to happiness, misery being the sure attendant of a woman without virtue; she loves it, as dear to her respectable father and tender mother. These sentiments inspire her with a degree

gree of enthusiasm, that elevates her soul and subdues every irregular appetite.

Of the absent she never talks but with circumspection, her female acquaintance especially. She has remarked, that what renders women prone to detraction, is talking of their own sex; and that they are more equitable with respect to ours. Sophia therefore never talks of women, but to express the good she knows of them: of others she says nothing.

WITHOUT much knowledge of the world, she is attentive, obliging and graceful in all she does. A good disposition does more for her, than much art does for others. She possesses a degree of politeness, which, void of ceremony, proceeds from a desire to please, and which consequently never fails to please.

THE next portrait is of a fine woman drawn by the celebrated Earl of Chesterfield.

LET

LET Flavia be their model, who, though she could support any character, assumes none; is never misled by fancy or vanity, but guided singly by reason. Whatever she says or does, is the manifest result of a happy nature, and a good understanding; though she knows whatever women ought, and it may be more than they are required to know. She conceals the superiority she has, with as much care as others take to display the superiority they have not: she conforms herself to the turn of the company she is in, but in a way of rather avoiding to be distanced, than desiring to take the lead. Are they merry, she is chearful; are they grave, she is serious; are they absurd, she is silent. Though she thinks and speaks as a man would do, she effeminates, if I may use the expression, whatever she says, and adds all the graces of her own sex to the strength of ours. She is well bred without the troublesome ceremonies and

A a   frivolous

frivolous forms of thofe who only affect to be fo. As her good breeding proceeds jointly from good nature and good fenfe, the former inclines her to oblige, and the latter fhows her the eafieft and beft way of doing it. Women's beauty like men's wit, is generally fatal to the owners, unlefs directed by a judgment that feldom accompanies a great degree of either. Her beauty feems but a proper and decent lodging for fuch a mind. She knows the true value of it; and far from thinking that it authorifes impertinence and coquetry, it redoubles her care to avoid thofe errors that are its ufual attendants. Thus, fhe not only unites in herfelf all the advantages of body and mind, but even reconciles contradictions in others; for fhe is loved and efteemed, though envied by all.

I shall add but one character more, which is that of the Duchefs of Guife, penned

penned by the Duc de Sully, a moft complete female character in my opinion.

In any age that has not loft every diftinction between virtue and vice, the Duchefs of Guife would univerfally have been held the chief of her fex, for the qualities of her heart and mind. Every branch of her conduct was regulated by a native rectitude of foul: fhe had not even the idea of evil, either in advifing or acting. Her difpofition was at the fame time fo fweet, as never to feel the flighteft emotion of hatred, malignity, envy, nor even of ill humour. No other woman ever poffeffed fo many graces of converfation; nor, to a wit fo fubtile and refined, added a more perfect fimplicity of manners. The pleafing as well as more elevated qualities, were fo happily blended in her compofition, that fhe was at once tender and lively, tranquil and gay.

SECT.

SECT. VII.

EDUCATION *with respect to* RELIGION.

THE most delicate branch of education, is that which concerns religion. All human beings have an innate sense of right and wrong, by means of which children are susceptible of moral instruction. They listen to an interesting story, take an affection to those who behave well, and an aversion to those who behave ill. Such exercise, which moulds the heart to virtue, has one peculiar advantage, that it is highly agreeable: children never tire of it*. Children are equally

---

* The following little story is so sweet and interesting, that I am fond of any pretext to introduce it; and my pretext is, that it is an additional proof of the sense of right and wrong being innate; though that fact is so firmly established in the opinion of every rational person, as to render any new evidence very little necessary. A female child was born deaf and dumb. At four years of age, when her parents were

equally fufceptible of inftruction with regard to natural religion. The being of

were clearly fenfible of her defect, they fent her to a boarding fchool at Briftol; and left her there for years, without providing either for board or cloaths. The father, who died a few years ago, left his wife and fon in good circumftances, with L. 1000 to each of his younger children, the fame fum to his dumb daughter in cafe fhe fhould come to the ufe of fpeech; otherways an annuity only of L. 30, to commence when fhe fhould be of age. Since the father's death, fhe was vifited by her brothers and fifters, but without any mark of affection, not a fingle word about the board either from mother or children. So much upon the dark fide of the profpect. Now to the bright fide. Sophia, which is the young woman's name, is of fo mild and amiable a difpofition, that the boarding miftreffes have adopted her for their daughter. Their claim is confiderable for board, cloaths, and education; but they forbear fuing for it, left the young woman fhould be taken from them. In needle-work, drawing, dancing, and mimicry, fhe excels. But what only is to the prefent point, her miftreffes vouch upon every occafion, that her ideas of juftice and moral rectitude are extremely correct, and that her practice is entirely conformable to them. Ideas of right and wrong may be improved by education; but without a foundation in nature, an attempt to inculcate them would be no lefs unfuccefsful, than an attempt to give an idea of colour to one born blind.

of a God and the worship due to him, being engraved on the mind, make a branch of our nature. As nature thus takes the lead, it is the duty of parents to second nature. They ought to inculcate into their children, that God is their friend and heavenly Father; and that they ought to perform his will, which is to do all the good they can. Convince them that God is always present, and that not a thought can be concealed from him. Accompany every one of your lessons with describing the Deity as benevolent and humane, wishing the good of his creatures, and rewarding the virtuous, if not in this life, assuredly in a life to come *.

As this is a capital branch of education, indeed the most capital, it merits great attention. It is easy to fortify in children

* See Sketches of the History of Man. Second Edit. vol. 4. page 359.

children the belief of a Deity, becaufe his exiftence is engraved on the human heart; but it is not eafy to fortify that belief, fo as to become a ruling principle of action. And yet this is indifpenfable; for belief without producing that effect, is of little fignificancy with refpect to the duties of religion, which are the great and ultimate end of inftruction. In order that a firm belief of the Deity may warm the mind to perfevere in what is right, the following hints may be of ufe to parents and tutors. Take proper opportunities of talking pleafantly to your children of their heavenly Father, who loves them, and who, though unfeen, is always doing them good; that he created the fun to warm them, and made the earth to produce every thing neceffary for their nourifhment and for their cloathing. In fine weather, lead them to the fields, and point out to them the various beauties of nature. " How beautiful that fmooth

" plain

" plain interfected with a stream perpe-
" tually flowing; how comfortable to the
" eye its verdure, and how beneficial by
" giving food to many innocent and use-
" ful animals! Behold that gay parterre,
" variegated with a thousand sweet co-
" lours. See that noble oak spreading its
" branches all around, affording a shade
" in summer, and shelter in winter. Li-
" sten to the birds which chear us with
" their music, and are busily employed
" in bringing forth their young." Im-
press it upon the minds of your children, that all these things are contrived by our heavenly Father to make us happy; and that it ought to be our chief delight to testify upon all occasions our gratitude to him.

When a child has behaved well, fail not to let it know, that it has given pleasure to its heavenly Father, and that he will reward it when he sees proper. In sickness,

sickness, exhort it to suffer patiently; because it is in the hands of God, who will do what is best for it. If this chearful doctrine be carefully instilled into the hearts of children, they will acquire a habit of considering the Deity in the amiable light of a friend and benefactor, who never will forsake them.

But though it is necessary to describe the Deity, not only as a friend to the good, but as an enemy to the wicked; be in no hurry with the latter, nor let it be mentioned till the benevolence of the Deity be deeply rooted in the mind of your children. When they are duly prepared, describe him as loath to punish, ready to forgive those who repent, an enemy to hardened sinners only; that he is angry indeed at children who misbehave, but that so are their parents; that good children are not afraid of their parents;

rents; and as little reason have they to be afraid of their heavenly Parent.

Religious education thus carried on, instead of inspiring gloominess and despondence, will contribute more than any other means to serenity of mind and chearfulness of temper. I zealously recommend this sort of discipline to parents, knowing that it is not sufficiently attended to. Surely, any frightful notion of the Deity, must have a dismal effect on a tender mind, susceptible of every impression, that of fear above all. Man formerly was thought to be of a nature so perverse, as to be governed by fear only, never by affection; and our Maker accordingly was represented as severe and unforgiving. The dread thus inspired into young persons, produces naturally abject superstition in a weak mind; and in the bold and thoughtless, a total neglect of religion. As the latter character is the more common,

mon, it cannot be surprising to find among us a neglect of religious duties prevailing so generally.

Stories contrived to fortify rational notions of the Deity, would have a good effect on children of nine or ten; the history, for example, of a young woman who never did a thing of moment, without first considering whether it would be agreeable to her Maker; who by that means led a chearful and innocent life, and was beloved by all; or the history of a young man, who, seduced by a train of temptations, lost sight of his Maker, and plunged headlong into vice. After a debauch, he dreamed that God, appearing with an angry countenance, threatned a severe punishment. He started from sleep in extreme agony: his wicked courses stared him in the face: he prayed ardently for pardon, and made a vow never again to lose sight of his Maker. The remainder

remainder of his life was no less exemplary for goodness, than the former part for vice. The lively impression of God's presence and superintendence, promoted by such histories, will guard against vice more effectually, than the actual presence of the most awful person on earth. A man so educated, will as little think of hiding his intentions from his Maker, as of hiding them from himself.

Considering how liable children are to the absurd impressions of ghosts and apparitions, can it be thought that they will be less open to the impression of the Deity, which has a solid foundation in nature? Examples are many of a connection so intimate between two friends, as that the image of the predeceased was always present to the survivor, rejoicing with him in prosperity, and comforting him in adversity. Surely, we are susceptible of a connection with our Maker, equally

equally intimate. I have often experienced the force of early impressions in trivial matters, far less apt than the presence of the Deity to occupy the mind. In the morning between sleeping and waking, I frequently imagine myself to be in the bed-chamber I occupied during childhood, the door here, the window there, very different from the form of my present bed-chamber: nor am I undeceived, till perfectly awake. From the window of my study looking to the fields in a reverie, the sight of a tree, resembling one in my original habitation, has frequently made me think myself to be there; so as even to contradict my eyesight, by substituting, instead of the present prospect, the one I had been accustomed to during my tender years. As more than half a century has elapsed since my infancy, these facts show clear- that early impressions never are obli-

It is true, that I have nothing
for

for these facts but my own evidence; but, as nature is the same in all, I take it for granted that similar instances have occurred to many.

Young persons duly initiated in the comforts of religion, hold their Maker to be their firmest friend, and their most powerful protector. They retire to private devotion, with the alacrity of one who goes to visit a bosom friend; and the hours that pass in that exercise, are remembered with entire satisfaction. In every difficulty they apply to their Maker: they pray to him in affliction; and in prosperity they pour out their grateful heart to him. Parents! attend above all other concerns to the education of your children: riches and honours are as nothing in comparison. It is in your power to stamp on their ductile mind, so deep an impression of a benevolent Deity, as to become their ruling principle of action.

tion. What praise do you not merit, if succefsful: what reproach, if negligent? I have a firm conviction, that if a due impreffion of the Deity be not fufficient to ftem the tide of corruption in an opulent and luxurious nation, it is vain to attempt a remedy *.

WHEN

---

* I can have no doubt but that the following letter upon this fubject, will be as agreeable to the public, as it was to me.

"I am very glad to hear, that you again have taken
"up your pen for the public fervice; efpecially as
"you begin at that feafon on which the whole har-
"veft of life depends. We, who are farmers, know
"the ground muft be tilled, cleaned, and good feed
"carefully fown, if we mean to reap a rich crop. I
"am proud to find, I have always followed your plan
"of religion, with the infants that have been under
"my care. Whenever they have admired the fun's
"refulgent beams, the lovely orb of the moon, or
"any of the ftriking beauties of nature, I have en-
"deavoured to raife their thoughts to the great Crea-
"tor, and to fet before them his Majefty, without
"the terrors that might drive them from the con-
"templation. In their feafons of recreation and
"innocent delights, I have reprefented him as the
"indulgent parent, from whofe bounty they enjoyed
"fuch

When your children, by regular training, come to have a warm sense of devotion, then is the time for entering them into the exercise of prayer. Teach them to pray for their parents, for their relations, and above all, that God will preserve them from doing ill. Say your prayers before them shortly and pathetically: they will imitate you without compulsion. But prescribe not at first regular hours; which to very young creatures

" such blessings, and who at all times can bestow
" every good, and guard from pain and evil. The
" fear of God is the beginning of wisdom; but the
" love of God is the parent of devotion. When, as
" men, they go forth into the world, and tempta-
" tions throng around them, they ought then to con-
" sider God in the awful character of a legislator,
" carefully to obey his laws, and to dread the displea-
" sure that must be the consequence of disobedience
" to laws on which the general welfare depends; no
" less in fact, though not so apparently, than on the
" regular course of the tides, or succession of the sea-
" sons. Nor will this any way impair the early prin-
" ciple of the love of God: for the more benevolent
" the lawgiver is, the more strictly will he require
" obedience to laws upon which our happiness de-
" pends."

creatures prove irkfome and fatiguing. Encourage them, however, to acquaint you when they have performed that duty. After being thus fairly initiated in an agreeable practice, it will not be difficult to introduce gradually more regularity. Let them know that regularity will prevent neglect and remiffnefs, which cannot fail to be a burden on their fpirits; that the morning and the evening are the moft proper times; the former to thank their Maker for the light of a new day, and to befeech him not to leave them to themfelves; the latter to attribute it to him if they have behaved well, and to beg pardon if they have done any thing amifs.

But I reft here, purpofing at the end of this fection, to prefent the reader with an illuftration of this fubject by another hand. I reckon upon fuffering by the comparifon; but I renounce felfifh views for the fake of my fellow citizens.

WHAT remains with respect to religious education, is to add a few hints upon revealed religion. This may be thought an extreme delicate point; because in endeavouring to instruct young people in the revelation that ought to be embraced, there may be danger of leading them astray. As revealed religion is not stamped on the heart, but requires profound reasoning, and the knowledge of many obscure facts, we are apt to conclude that it ought to be delayed till the faculty of reason be ripe; which resolves in leaving every person to judge for themselves. But this opinion ought not to be adopted; for as the generality of men are incapable to judge of a matter so intricate, they must be led. Now, I say, that it is better for them to be led in their younger years by a kindly parent or tutor, than to be left to form an opinion afterward as chance shall direct. For this reason, I am clear that children be educated in the religion established or tolerated by law.

law. Nor ought this to be confidered as a rafh conceffion; for fure I am, that ninety-nine of a hundred have no better foundation to build their faith upon. It may be demanded then, where lies the merit of a Chriftian above a Mahometan or a Pagan? I admit, that it cannot lie in following blindly the religion of one's anceftors. But as the Chriftian revelation is the moft perfect of all, and the pureft in its doctrines, it is highly meritorious in a Turk or a Pagan, who feeks truth with a fincere heart, to become a true Chriftian. At the fame time, I am far from thinking, that Chriftianity is the only road to heaven. All who have a good heart with a clear confcience, will meet with the fame reward. It is not material in the fight of the Almighty, whether the religion they have been taught is or is not orthodox, provided they be fincere. People follow naturally and innocently the faith of their parents; and the generality have no other means for

for embracing a revelation, real or pretended. How few are there who can depend on their own judgment, in making a choice! Are people to be condemned for judging wrong, who cannot judge at all? To me therefore it appears evidently the will of God, that sincerity should be the only title to his favour, leaving men to their own belief.

It may well be considered by us as a singular favour of Providence, that we enjoy the Christian Revelation, the purest and most luminous of all that have been given to men. With regard however to people ignorant of Christianity, it tends greatly to their peace of mind, to adhere to the religion established among them. Therefore, whatever unlucky doubts or scruples may haunt a man with respect to that religion, he ought to conceal them from his children. In a Christian country, let him employ all honest means to breed

breed his children sincere Christians. To that end, among other particulars more material, a set of prints representing the history of the Old and New Testament, will contribute greatly. Young creatures delight in pictures; and by that means, the material facts relative to Christianity may be deeply stamped on their minds, leaving when they grow up, little inclination to doubt of their reality.

HERE indeed I zealously exhort parents and teachers to guard against bigotry and superstition, which, if early sown in young minds, are not easily rooted out. Teach your children to prefer their own religion; but inculcate at the same time, that the virtuous are acceptable to God, however erroneous in point of belief. Press it home on them, that there is nothing in nature to hinder different sects of Christians from living amicably together, more than different
sects

sects of philosophers, or of men who work in different arts; especially as the articles of faith that distinguish these sects are purely speculative: they have no relation to morals, nor any influence on our conduct. Yet from these distinctions have proceeded rancour and animosity, as if our most important concerns had been at stake. In a different view, the absurdity appears still more glaring. These articles, the greater part at least, relate to subjects beyond the reach of human understanding; so that no man can say whether they are true or false. The Almighty, by his works of creation, has made his wisdom and benevolence manifest: but he has not found it necessary to explain to his creatures the manner of his existence; and in all appearance the manner of his existence is beyond the reach of our conceptions. Yet in a creed commonly ascribed to Athenasius, the manner of God's existence is handled

dled with the same air of certainty, as if it were contained in a divine revelation. Certain it is, that the propositions laid down in that creed, are far beyond the reach of human knowledge. I forbear to mention, that the greater part of them, if they have any distinct meaning, contradict common sense. And yet, good God! what oceans of blood have been shed by the inveteracy of the orthodox against the Arians, occasioned chiefly by that very creed; men massacring one another without remorse, and even without pity—more cruel far than beasts of prey, who never kill but for food. Persecution for the sake of religion, would have been entirely prevented by wholesome education, instilling into the minds of young people, that difference in opinion is no just cause of discord; and that different sects may live amicably together. In a word, neglect no opportunity to impress on the mind of your pupils, that religion

is

is given for our good; and that no religion can be true which tends to disturb the peace of society.

APPENDIX to SECTION VII.

ART. I.

THAT the sense of Deity is innate has been shewn elsewhere *. The present enquiry is how to unfold it.

The perception of our own existence is quickly followed by that of the existence of God; or rather, they grow up together. The pleasures of novelty and beauty and grandeur are early felt; it seems possible to excite, even in the minds of children, a reflection on the author of those pleasures. Children are indebted to their parents for food and clothes and other comforts,

* Sketches of the History of Man. Edit. 2. vol. 4. page 190.

comforts, and they feel gratitude and attachment. But who makes the sun to rise, and the flowers to grow, and fruit to ripen? They are the questions of children, the seed of an answer is in their own mind, it only needs to be unfolded. By beginning here, the first idea of God is that of a benevolent Being, and the first devout sentiments are those of gratitude and admiration.

GLOOMY views of the Supreme Being, and of the service which he requires, have the worst effect on the minds of youth. The celebrated Boyle, when a young man, visited the scenes of St Bruno's solitude. The stories and pictures of that Saint overwhelmed him with melancholy. The misery of his creatures seemed to be the sacrifice which God required. According to his own account, " nothing but " the forbiddenness of self-dispatch pre- " vented his acting it."

It is not meet to burden young minds with religious instruction. If it be conveyed in the form of a task, it will soon grow irksome. If it consist in definitions of God and explanations, it will probably amount to the knowledge of words. If abstruse and inadequate reasonings be used, they will choke the good seed which you mean to cherish.

In unfolding a truth which affects the imagination and the heart, proper seasons must be chosen. When the sun rises from the sea, and dispels the clouds, and gilds the mountains, while birds sing and the air is fragrant; you may aid your pupil's contemplation on that power which daily renews our joy. In the silence and solemnity of a starry night, his thoughts ascend to the Creator. While it thunders, he readily perceives that reverence is due to the Almighty.

There are seasons when the doctrine of providence, and of immortality, a branch of that doctrine, may be deeply impressed. Recoveries and escapes and deliverances are often experienced in youth; when your pupil has experienced any of these, with the slightest aid he will recognise a providence. Your disease was extreme, the physician gave no hope, your companion was carried to the grave. What power restored you to your sorrowing friends? what gratitude is due to that power? what love to those friends who took so deep an interest in your affliction? You have escaped an accident which the next moment had proved fatal. Who preserved your life? for what end was it preserved?

Marcus Antoninus was thankful to Providence that his mother recovered from a sickness which had like to have cut her off in her youth. Such an interposition duly

duly weighed, leaves a more powerful and permanent impression than profound reasoning, and awakens a livelier gratitude. Those who have cultivated piety, and like Antoninus recorded its progress, have all been touched with early interpositions of Providence, and treasured them up as memorials of Divine Goodness and grounds of hope.

Youth seldom passes without a time to weep. The death-bed of a parent or of a young friend, melts the heart. Concern and attachment grow as the hour approaches. Death leaves him inconsolable. Immortality is the source of consolation, and now is the time to open it. It accords with lively sorrow, which clings to a departed friend, and dwells on the thought of an everlasting union. Divine Goodness, which the shadow of death had veiled, shines forth again. Were dying parents, like the late Lady Cathcart,

cart, to awaken a sense of God and immortality in the minds of children, it would make an indelible impression.

The doctrines of Providence and a future state, interest all mankind. Systems of education which overlook them are very deficient. The reasonings of Theologians and Sceptics, may have given to an important science a discouraging aspect. With them it may still be left to dispute with Clarke and Dodwell, and to trace the intricacies of Spinoza; but in a system of education suited to man, his relation to God, with the sentiments and duties founded on that relation, is an essential branch. The steps by which your pupil advances in knowledge, all lead to the Creator. By giving them this direction, improvement and delight will mingle.

A R T.

ART. II.

THERE is an early tendency to contemplate the works of nature, and to enquire. If the inclination and capacity of youth were consulted, natural history would be the first branch of education. On this subject, the pupil is introduced with ease and pleasure to industry and thought. Curiosity is gratified and excited by turns. A way of knowledge is opened in the desert, and a path in the deep waters. Final causes are perceived, and views of wisdom open. He is introduced to communion with God.

Much depends on the method in which natural history is taught. The sophistry of materialism darkens the understanding, and chills the heart, and damps the ardour of pursuit. The sense of Deity, which the mere detail of facts would

would cherish, is blasted by cold and captious reasoning; the result is doubt and melancholy, perhaps indolence and sensuality. But when marks of wise and beneficent design are pointed out, the detail of facts becomes more interesting. Reason is exercised. Admiration is felt. The heart warms at every new prospect of benevolence. Fresh ardour kindles in a pursuit by which the highest feelings of the mind are gratified.

If the inclination and capacity of the pupil be still consulted, experimental philosophy is the next step. It contributes to the arts of life, and it may likewise contribute to the knowledge of God. " It " gives a relish, as Mr Boyle observed " and felt, for abstract truths which do " not gratify ambition, sensuality or low " interests." The laws of nature suppose a Lawgiver. The properties of body, subjected to the power and ingenuity and use of man, lead to the Author of these properties and of this subjection. The doctrine of cause and effect is explained. The metaphysical dust is easily wiped off. With intuitive conviction, the mind rests in a first cause, independent and self-existent. It rests in silent awe. The explanations of schoolmen are blasphemy.

THE sciences acquire new importance and dignity, and reflect new honour on their professors, as they dispel superstition and establish faith in the perfections and providence of God. " Our views of " nature," says M'Laurin, an eminent and enlightened teacher, " however im- " perfect, serve to represent to us in the " most sensible manner, that mighty " power which prevails throughout, act- " ing with a force and efficacy that ap- " pears to suffer no diminution from the " greatest distances of space or intervals " of time; and that wisdom which we
" see

" see equally displayed in the exquisite
" structure and just motions of the great-
" est and subtilest parts. These, with
" perfect goodness by which they are
" evidently directed, constitute the su-
" preme object of the speculations of a
" philosopher, who, while he contem-
" plates and admires so excellent a system,
" cannot but be himself excited and ani-
" mated to correspond with the general
" harmony of nature." Sir Isaac Newton concludes his principal works with thoughts of God, sublime in proportion to the objects which filled his mind, and the clearness with which he viewed them. In a late Essay on Gravitation, an idea is presented of some centre of the universe unspeakably remote, round which the sun and stars may gravitate. After supporting the hypothesis by analogy, and by the change of place actually observed in many stars, it thus concludes, " What
" an astonishing thing is this when con-
" sidered

"sidered in its proper and full extent!
"It seems the voice of nature reaching
"from the uttermost heavens, inviting
"us to enlarge and elevate our views."

ART. III.

FROM the knowledge of external things, the mind is conducted to the knowledge of itself: a brighter display of the Deity opens. Human wisdom appears in mechanical arts, but still more in the arts of government. The laws of motion in matter, and of instinct in brutes are suited to their subjects; but the laws which regulate a mind capable of thinking and chusing, lead to more profound researches. The labour is difficult, but the recompense is great. In tracing these laws we discover the end of our creation, and the means of attaining it. We discover hidden treasures of Divine

vine Wisdom, in a subject of higher dignity and more exquisite workmanship, than the material world. We feel a principle of justice and kind affection, which aid our conceptions of the Divine Justice and Benevolence. Some of the passions find an object in God; and moral excellence attracts the heart.

The principles of taste are the easiest and most pleasant branch of human nature; and with them, perhaps, it is fittest to begin. The pleasures of imagination are relished in youth: as their sources are traced with the means of purifying them, they acquire a new relish. Means fitted to their ends in so complicated a machine as man, display profound wisdom: when these ends are so many delicious pleasures, they renew the impression of Divine Benevolence. The benevolence of God is the foundation of piety, and it cannot be laid too deep. While the

pleasures

pleasures of imagination are enjoyed, gratitude may at times be roused. Many of these pleasures accord with devotion, and rise in the exercise of it to their highest note. Great and awful and immeasurable objects are sublime; as they raise the thoughts to God, the mind swells with still more exalted pleasure. The enthusiasm of poetry is felt, and the fire of devotion burns. Hymns to the Creator were early expressions of piety among men, and piety may still be cherished in early years by songs of praise.

Laws which regulate conduct, are more important than those by which pleasure is dispensed.

Kind affections spring up in youth; it is the season for rearing the amiable virtues. Pleasure accompanies every act of goodness; the gratitude which it excites, and the praise which it attracts, heighten

heighten that pleasure; devotion purifies and exalts it. Benevolence, which is animated by views of Divine Benevolence, and works together with God, is pure and permanent; it is proof against ingratitude and unmerited reproach.

While justice is explained, the obligation is felt, and the sanctions which enforce it. Human laws are contemplated as a part of God's administration, founded on the sense of justice which he has given, inflicting punishments which that sense approves, and establishing order in society. So far the prospect is bright. But your pupil must be instructed in the disorder which actually prevails, the imperfection of human laws, the partiality and deceivableness of judges, the triumphs of iniquity. A cloud gathers on the prospect. Indignation rises at the view of oppression, and sympathy with the oppressed, and an appeal to that Being who

who made man upright. Immortality, opened through the vale of death, it opens again through the vale of iniquity.

If difficulties occur in comparing the justice of God with his benevolence, the following hints by Muralt are submitted.

" The faculties with which man is
" endowed, tend, when properly exer-
" cised, to the perfection of his nature.
" When they are turned from their true
" destination, disorder ensues, great in
" proportion to the excellence of the fa-
" culties perverted. The order which
" subsists among the members of the
" body is essential, not only to its per-
" fection, but to its happiness. Disor-
" der in any member of the body, is
" notified by pain; disorder in the fa-
" culties of the mind, is in like manner
" notified by pain of mind. Pain is the
" consequence

" confequence of diforder, the neceffary
" unavoidable confequence; were it o-
" therways, both body and mind would
" go to ruin. Detach the idea of feve-
" rity from the juftice of God: were
" creatures free from diforder, that fe-
" verity would not exift. The effential
" juftice of God, is his approbation of
" that order which renders intelligent
" creatures happy; and of confequence,
" a difapprobation of the diforder which
" renders them miferable. The feem-
" ing feverity of his juftice, is a con-
" ftant and preffing call to return to hap-
" pinefs, and to that order with which
" it is neceffarily connected. The ju-
" ftice, which feems fevere in its effects,
" is, in its principle, goodnefs directed by
" wifdom. The principle by which he
" confents to the pain of his creatures,
" is the fame by which he wills them to
" be happy."

REASON

REASON is of late growth: much muſt be done in the way of diſcipline before it can be applied: that diſcipline, however, ſhould be adapted to reaſon, which is hereafter to review it. Beware of conveying to your pupil religious principles that will not ſtand the teſt of enquiry; when he comes to winnow them, the wheat may fly off with the chaff. In a dark age, prejudices friendly to virtue may operate through life; but when light ruſhes in, the foundation of piety and virtue may be ſhaken. Eraſmus obſerved, that all the reformers he was acquainted with, became worſe men than they were before. The firſt reformers, in renouncing venerable prejudices with which the moſt important truths were mingled, underwent a ſevere trial; nor is it much to be wondered at, if, in breaking the bands of ſuperſtition, the bands of love were looſed. The children of proteſtants acknowledged no authority

thority but scripture, and they escaped the trial of their fathers. In the progress of enquiry, scripture came to be judged by reason, the moral sense, and the sense of Deity. In this state of things, it seems prudent to begin with incontrovertible essential truths, and to prepare and cultivate reason for judging of the rest.

ART. IV.

WHEN the sense of Deity is unfolded, and reason cultivated, it is time to judge of revelation. Christianity claims attention on several accounts: it is the religion of our fathers: it has a shew of evidence: if it be true, it is a truth of high concern.

Many of the objections to Christianity are owing to misrepresentations of it. Let the New Testament be consulted. Does it ascribe to God a character worthy the Creator of the universe and the Father of men? Does it clear and extend the view of his wisdom and benevolence? Does it make the way to communion with him more plain and pleasant?

Is the appointment of a Mediator analogous to the ways of Providence, expressive of Divine Condescension, and suited to human nature? Is it consoling to the heart under a sense of guilt, to be assured of pardon? Does moral excellence made perfect by suffering, seem to be a sacrifice which God will accept? Is it natural to the mind of man, to feel admiration and love at the view of moral excellence, and yield to its transforming influence?

TAKE a view of man in his low estate. Think if it be godlike to send glad tidings to the poor, if it be godlike to console

sole the miserable, and if the sympathy of an affectionate and powerful friend be a strong consolation? Man is mortal, and Jesus passed before us through death, not with an awful insensibility, which leaves the feeling heart behind.

Does the doctrine of a resurrection fall in with our predilection for these bodies, and open as it were to the eye of sense the prospect of immortality? And does the doctrine of judgment accord with the natural feeling, that we are accountable?

Do the sufferings of Christ, and the glory which followed, illustrate and ratify his important doctrine of a state of trial, preparatory to a state of retribution?

Judge Christianity by its effects. Does it kindle love to God and man, and establish

blish the authority of conscience, and reconcile man to his lot?

If your child be satisfied that Christ is a teacher sent from God, and is willing to be his disciple, it is meet to confess him before men. The celebration of his death is a proper testimony of regard. Such a Benefactor deserves to be had in everlasting remembrance.

The hearts of the young, when first introduced to communion with the faithful, are accessible and soft. Parents might avail themselves of this season to recal their early dedication to God, to explain the wisdom and love which inspired the discipline through which they have been made to pass, to foretel its influence on their future conduct, to anticipate the time when that conduct shall be judged, and to devolve the care of it on themselves.

ART.

ART V.

WHILE other paſſions are ſpringing up, and attended to with a wiſe and watchful eye, the devout paſſions claim a ſhare in that attention.

The works of God inſpire humility. When we look up to the heavenly bodies, and meditate the extent and the number and the glory of them; we return to ourſelves with lowly thoughts. " Lord " what is man that thou art mindful of " him?"

Perfect innocence is not the portion of mortality. Even in worthy purſuits the judgment may err, and in the exerciſe of right affections the heart may wander. In youth a paſſion may break its bounds, and for a moment lay waſte the ſoul. Remorſe is felt. Under its ſevere and awful preſſure, the ſoul returns

turns to God, and melts in penitential sorrow. The peace which begins to dawn, is a token of the Divine compassion. The fruits of this exercise are a lively sense of the danger of guilt, the humbleness of mind which becomes an imperfect creature, and sympathy with those who are in the same imperfect state. The devout act passes in retirement betwixt the soul and God; but the fruits of it you may aid your young friend to cultivate.

Love to God is excited and cherished by reflecting on his favours, and on the goodness from whence they flow. Affection to a creature must be limited, but unmixed and unbounded goodness is the object of unbounded affection. The heart does not rest in any human enjoyment, but it rests in God; the object is adequate and the enjoyment complete. Divine love attracts the ardour and sensibility

bility of youth, and averts debasing passions.

First feelings are critical; by them the character is often decided. Suppose them sensual; how deep they sink! how often renewed by a polluted imagination, and how fondly cherished! They become the hidden treasure of the heart, to which it retires for a dark selfish evanescent joy: the presence of the virtuous cannot always suppress them, nor the gate of the sanctuary shut them out. The path of honour is for ever abandoned. Early impressions of piety in like manner take possession of the heart. The first feelings of devotion are remembered with delight. God is sought and he is found in the outgoings of the morning, in delightful and in awful scenes, in the peace and in the tumults of nations, in the inmost recesses of the soul. When the mind is unoccupied, it is drawn by love to the Father

ther of mercies. Love to God brightens the sunshine of prosperity, and perfumes with sweet incense the sacrifices which are made to virtue. Every thing praiseworthy is to be expected from the youth who loves his Creator and acts as under his eye.

Divine love has at times appeared in a less inviting form. Unfeeling men, like Dr Clarke, alarmed at the effects of enthusiasm, have denied the existence of any affection or passion of which God is the object. Dr Butler, with a deeper insight into human nature in his sermon on the love of God, has established the doctrine on its true foundation. The success of enthusiasts in ages of ignorance, and among the ignorant of the present age, denotes a principle in the human mind which corresponds to their instructions. It is a sacred principle, and deserves to be be called forth and cherished by the voice of wisdom.

MADAME Guyon taught the ladies of Lewis the Fourteenth's degenerate Court, to love their Creator. The young yielded to her persuasive eloquence. She was accused of corrupting the youth. Her defence was in the spirit of her instructions. " But the youth whom I have corrupted, " thou knowest, O my God, are full of " love to thee." The error of pure love, if it must be accounted an error, was yet honourable for human nature. Like the Stoic philosophy of old, it gave to the world characters of sublime and godlike virtue. The names of St Francis de Sales and Fenelon, like those of Epictetus and Antoninus, are lights shining in a dark place. In the midst of degeneracy, they are pleasing memorials that God made man after his own image.

ART. VI.

POLITICS is the last branch of education. Its theory illustrates the principles of virtue and religion. The study of government and laws extends the view of moral obligation; the student feels his relation to the public, and meditates the duties of a citizen. The history of nations, with the causes of their rise and fall, extends the view of Providence.

The art of rising in life is at last the object. Concerning politics in this sense, Lord Bacon observes, and perhaps the observation was verified in himself, that "unless the young be instructed in re-"ligious and moral principles before "they proceed to politics, they are apt "to account moral differences unreal, "and to measure all things by utility "and success." In the career of ambition,

bition, religion is a bulwark against surrounding temptation. Means suggested by friends, and authorised by example, and crowned with success, and adorned with Chesterfield's eloquence, are reviewed by conscience. Figure and fortune appear light when laid in the balance with modesty and uprightness. The steps of a religious youth may not be marked with shining honours, but they will never be stained by insincerity. A sense of the Divine presence, become habitual and pleasant, insures uprightness.

In Roman Catholic countries there are houses of spiritual retreat, where the well disposed retire at times to commune with God and with their own hearts. A public institution of this kind may seem ostentatious, but the spirit of it is laudable. In the busiest life a day may be found for sacred solitude. The youth who has acquired a relish for the pleasures fures of devotion, yields his heart to thofe pleafures. He views, at a proper diftance, the active life upon which he has entered, and makes a true eftimate of wealth and fame and pre-eminence. He attends to his character as an accountable being, and thinks of the time when fuccefs or difappointment will figure lefs than the steps by which they arrived; when the pleafure of fuccefs will be increafed by the honourable means of attaining it, and the pain of difappointment leffened, becaufe nothing difhonourable was done to avert it. The particular duties of his fphere are reviewed: if the review prefents imperfections, he does not difguife them to his own mind, nor does he check humility. Under the impreffion of divine goodnefs, he learns to forgive himfelf, and to improve the experience of former errors againft future temptation. Plans of ufefulnefs are devifed, and kind affections cherifhed.

ed. The beauties of virtue open in prospect, and, like a traveller refreshed, he sets forward with alacrity.

The intercourse of friendship is a further mean of uprightness. Young men whose mutual attachment is dignified by principle, investigate together the fair and honourable course: self-deceit is unveiled, false shame is combated, and self-esteem is cherished. Religious conversation in mixed company was fashionable once, and it degenerated into hypocrisy; it now retires to the privacy of friendship, and resumes its charm. Truths which elevate the soul are canvassed and pondered. Generous affections flow and mingle. Existence is felt to be a blessing.

Attendance on public worship is a decent avowal of piety. In the solemn assembly, the distinction of ranks is suspended, mutual benevolence kindles, and the

the fire of devotion burns: the laws of God are heard with reverence. Though the effects of social worship be not always felt, through the distraction of the worshipper, or the incapacity of those who minister; still one of just and liberal sentiments will add the weight of his example to an institution, which, with all its imperfections, promotes a sense of God and of moral obligation among men.

ART. VII.

THE opinion of Rousseau, that religious instruction may be safely deferred till fifteen or even eighteen years of age, has weight perhaps with some parents and tutors, and contributes to the neglect of early piety. Rousseau's talents entitle him to a respectful hearing; but on a subject so important reasons ought to be weighed.

Appendix to Section VII.

HE alleges that " the idea which a " young mind forms of God is low and " unworthy of him." Will not this argument likewise conclude against teaching religion to the old? The best idea man can form of God, is in many respects low and unworthy of him. Still man is made to know his Creator, and to act in consequence of that knowledge. In teaching other sciences, we are not discouraged tho' the learner's first views be imperfect; we gradually present such as are more clear and extensive and satisfying. It is further to be considered, that in religion the heart is concerned as much as the understanding: affection may be sincere while reason is feeble. The first love of an innocent heart, is a sacrifice of a sweet favour.

HE alleges that " it is better to have " no ideas of God than such as are in- " jurious," and accommodates a saying
of

of Plutarch to his argument, " I would rather be forgotten, than remembered as unjuft, envious, jealous, and fo tyrannical as to exact more than I give means of accomplifhing." It were certainly better to be ignorant of God, than to think him unjuft and tyrannical; but is it then impoffible to convey to a young mind an idea of divine benevolence? Will not that idea be relifhed, while pleafure and hope combine to make the morning of life ferene; Is there a likelier mean of averting injurious thoughts of God, than prefenting fuch as are juft? A mind enlightened with views of the divine goodnefs, and touched with the participation of it, is prepared to meet with temporary evils, and to difcern goodnefs through the veil. Is a mind kept in ignorance of God till the ills of life arife and thicken in profpect, equally well prepared?

He labours to prove, what nobody doubts, that God will not punish involuntary ignorance. But is there no blame in voluntarily eftranging the young from piety? The importance of an early impreffion is acknowledged; Rouffeau acknowledged and illuftrated it in the cafe of compaffion. If love to men be promoted by exciting early and managing fkilfully fentiments of humanity, may not love to God be promoted by exciting and regulating devout fentiments, before the pleafures and cares of this life take poffeffion of the heart? Our author laments, that pleafures natural to the young and fuited to their years are with-held; and in the fpirit of philanthropy recommends to parents, that at whatever period God calls their children, they may not die without having tafted happinefs. Upon this principle, it feems unkind to withhold the pleafures of piety from the young. Even in the dawn of reafon, God is seen in his works, and felt in his favours; and well grounded hopes arise: the young can taste the pleasures of admiration, and praise, and trust. Youth is not exempted from calamity: when father and mother forsake them, they recognise the providence of a Father in heaven. Those who minister at death-bed, know that the young are susceptible of divine consolation; that under its sacred influence they suffer in patience, and comfort their weeping parents, and die in peace.

There are situations and events in human life, which call forth the religious principle: where it has been uncultivated, as is generally the case in high life, it appears in a forbidding form. Lewis the Fourteenth's education was neglected; his religion, when calamity called it forth, was made up of abject superstition and cruel bigotry, ruinous in proportion

to

to his power. The conversions of *eclat* as they are called in France, usually consist in a transition from the chambers of voluptuousness to the cells of St Ursula or St Bruno. Even in more enlightened countries, religion, operating late in an untutored mind, exhibits ostentatious sanctity and blind credulity; conscience, which ought to direct, submits to be directed,—a deposit too important to be entrusted with any creature. The religious principle, when duly cultivated, is a security against profaneness on the one hand, and fanaticism on the other; it brings forth the peaceable fruits of righteousness.

If religious instruction be neglected till the period marked by Rousseau, there is the utmost reason to fear that it will be for ever neglected. Your pupil must pass through life destitute of the surest guide; and he must pass through death destitute of all consolation.

A R T.

ART. VIII.

PRAYER.

THE propriety of prayer is seldom questioned, except by philosophers. Rousseau in a treatise on Education says, " I thank God for his favours, but I do " not pray to him. What should I ask?" He professes " not to philosophise with " his pupil, but to assist him in consult- " ing his own heart." And is there not in the heart a tendency to prayer strongly felt at times, as in danger that human power cannot avert, in perplexity from which human prudence cannot extricate, under sorrow for which this world yields no consolation, and under the pangs of an awakened conscience? Was it not a dictate of the heart which made the mothers of Israel bring their little children to Jesus, that he might lay his hands on them and pray?

Short forms of prayer are of use at first. The prayer which little children are taught to make for their father and their mother, may be considered as the beginning of piety and filial love, and a mean of unfolding them.

As children advance let the form be varied. Let it express a sense of dependence, gratitude, and desire to grow in favour with God and men. Fenelon's morning prayer, " Faites que nous com-" mencions aujourd'hui à nous corriger, " &c." supposes the work still to begin, it favours self-deceit and lukewarmness. The forms should be adapted to a progressive state.

Let prayer to God be made with reverence. Reverence may be felt, even before the object of it is distinctly apprehended. From that sympathetic reverence which the solemnities of worship excite,

excite, the mind gradually rises to an invisible object.

The preparation of the heart is necessary. It may be prepared by elevating views of nature. " The heavens declare " the glory of the Lord: they declare it " to all the inhabitants of the earth. " There is no speech nor language where " their voice is not heard. Their awful " and majestic silence speaks the language " of every people. It speaks to the heart " of man." Before that powerful and benign Majesty, let us bow and worship. Views of Providence may in like manner prepare the heart. " I wound and I " heal. I kill and I make alive." To that Being, in whose hand our life is, and who alone can make us happy, let us devote ourselves. Select passages of scripture may be used to predispose the heart. Prayer degenerates into rote, if the heart be not prepared.

WHILE

WHILE you pray with and for your children, the principles of devotion in their minds unfold. In that sacred hour, they feel themselves the objects of tender affection: they perceive that you are dependent as well as they, that blessings must be derived from a higher hand on yourselves and on them. " The remem-
" brance of many prayers offered up for
" them by their parents, draws to vir-
" tue. Even in foreign lands, and amidst
" busy scenes, the hearts of children
" melt at times with that affectionate re-
" membrance, and yield many soothing
" acknowledgments of the debt of love
" which they still owe. Even after pa-
" rents are laid in the dust, that remem-
" brance draws to virtue. Shall I trouble
" their rest by departing from innocence?
" Shall I frustrate the last strong desire
" which filled their spirits as they de-
" parted? Can I doubt that the favour
" of God extends to the children of his
" worshippers?

"worshippers? From the day that they forsook me, his favour hath compassed me about, it still encompasseth me*."

The stated and avowed exercise of devotion, is the only remedy against false shame: the strongest arguments cannot overcome it. Let parents who believe in the efficacy of prayer, and who are yet ashamed to pray, deliver their children from the same temptation.

When the habit of praying daily is acquired, devout thoughts associate with the hour of prayer. The impression of God's presence often renewed, checks temptation, and strengthens virtue, and establishes tranquillity of mind on a good foundation.

* A sermon by Mr Charteris, Minister of Wilton, on 1 Tim. ii. 1.

SECT. VIII.

INSTRUCTIONS *preparatory to the* MARRIED STATE.

PUBERTY, when new appetites and desires spring up, is the most critical time for education. Let the animal appetite be retarded as long as possible in both sexes. It is not difficult to keep females within bounds; for they are trained to reserve and to suppress their desires. As the same reserve enters not into the education of young men, extraordinary means must be used to keep them within bounds. Employ your male pupil in hunting or other violent exercise that engrosses him, and leaves no room for wandering thoughts. But when he cannot longer be restrained, then is the time for discoursing with him of marriage, for displaying its sweets, and for painting the distresses both of mind and body that result from a commerce with loose women. Give instances of such distresses; and describe them in vivid colours which at that ductile age will make a lasting impression.

Now is the precious time for lecturing your male pupil on the choice of a companion for life: no other branch of education is of deeper concern. Instil into his heart, that happiness in the married state, depends not on riches nor on beauty, but on good sense and sweetness of temper. Let him also keep in view, that in a married woman, the management of domestic affairs and the education of children, are indispensable duties. He will never tire of such conversation; and if he have any degree of sensibility, it will make such an impression as to guard him against a hasty choice. If not well guarded, he will probably

probably fall a prey to beauty or other external qualification, of little importance in the matrimonial ſtate. He ſets his heart on a pretty face, or a ſprightly air: he is captivated by a good ſinger or a nimble dancer; and his heated imagination beſtows on the admired object every perfection. A young man who has profited by the inſtructions given him, is not ſo eaſily captivated. The picture of a good wife is fixed in his mind; and he compares with it every young woman he ſees. "She is pretty, but has " ſhe good ſenſe? She has ſenſe, but is " ſhe well tempered? She dances ele- " gantly, or ſings with expreſſion; but " is ſhe not vain of ſuch trifles?" Judgment and ſagacity will produce a deliberate choice: love will come with marriage; and in that ſtate it makes an illuſtrious figure. After proper inſtruction, let the young man be at full liberty to chuſe for himſelf. In looking about where

where to apply, he cannot be better directed, than to a family where the parents and children live in perfect harmony, and are fond of one another. A young woman of such a family, seldom fails to make a good wife.

Beauty commonly is the first thing that attracts; and yet ought rather to be avoided in a wife. It is a dangerous property, tending to corrupt her mind, though it soon loses its influence over the husband. A figure agreeable and engaging, which inspires affection without the ebriety of love, is a much safer choice. The graces lose not their influence like beauty: at the end of thirty years, a virtuous woman who makes an agreeable companion, charms her husband perhaps more than at first. The comparison of love to fire holds good in one respect, that the fiercer it burns the sooner it is extinguished.

From the making choice of a wife we proceed to the making choice of a hufband. Mothers and nurfes are continually talking of marriage to their female pupils, long before it is fuggefted by nature; and it is always a great eftate, a fine coat, or a gay equipage that is promifed. Such objects impreffed on the mind of a child, will naturally bias her to a wrong choice when fhe grows up. Let her never hear of marriage but as proper for men and women: nature will fuggeft it to a young woman, perhaps fooner than fhe is capable of making a prudent choice. Neglect not at that time to talk to her of a comfortable companion for life. Let her know, that fhe will be defpifed if fhe marry below her rank; that happinefs however depends not on titles, nor on riches, but on the hufband's good temper, fobriety, and induftry, joined with a competency. At the fame time, to prevent a rafh choice, make it a frequent subject of conversation, that marriage is a hazardous step, especially for the female sex, as an error in chusing a husband admits of no remedy; that the duties of a married woman are burdensome, the comforts not always corresponding. Give her the history of prudent women, who, not finding a match to their liking, pass an easy independent life, much regarded by their friends and acquaintance. When a woman has given up the thoughts of matrimony, what employment more reputable can she have, than the education of young girls. Let her adopt for an heir a female child: she will soon feel the affection of a mother, especially if she make a discreet choice. A mother's affection commences, it is true, with the birth of her child; an affection, however, extremely slender, compared with what she feels afterward, from her watchful attention to its welfare, and from its suitable returns of gratitude

titude. A woman who adopts a promising child, has in that refpect every advantage that a mother enjoys. At any rate, the condition of a maiden lady with an adopted daughter, cannot in any view be thought inferior to that of a widow left with one or more children. I have the good fortune to be acquainted with three maiden ladies in high efteem, who have each of them undertaken the charge of a young orphan family. In all appearance, they live as happily as any widow; and affuredly more fo than many a married woman. Let it not however be thought, that I am edeavouring to diffuade young women from matrimony: it would be a flagitious as well as foolifh attempt. My purpofe only is to moderate a too violent appetite for it.

But now, fuppofing a young woman perfectly tractable, no means ought to be neglected for making her an ufeful and agreeable companion in the matrimonial ſtate. To make a good huſband, is but one branch of a man's duty; but it is the chief duty of a woman, to make a good wife. To pleaſe her huſband, to be a good œconomiſt, and to educate their children, are capital duties, each of which requires much training. Nature lays the foundation: diligence and ſagacity in the conductor, will make a beautiful ſuperſtructure. The time a girl beſtows on her doll, is a prognoſtic that ſhe will be equally diligent about her offspring.

WOMEN, deſtined by nature to be obedient, ought to be diſciplined early to bear wrongs, without murmuring. This is a hard leſſon; and yet it is neceſſary even for their own ſake: ſullenneſs or peeviſhneſs may alienate the huſband; but tend not to ſooth his roughneſs, nor to moderate his impetuoſity. Heaven made

made women infinuating, but not in order to be crofs: it made them feeble, not in order to be imperious: it gave them a fweet voice, not in order to fcold: it did not give them beauty, in order to disfigure it by anger.

But, after all, has nature dealt fo partially among her children, as to beftow on the one fex abfolute authority, leaving nothing to the other but abfolute fubmiffion? This indeed has the appearance of great partiality. But let us ponder a little.—Has a good woman no influence over her hufband? I anfwer, that that very fimple virtue of fubmiffion, can be turned to good account. A man indeed bears rule over his wife's perfon and conduct: his will is law. Providence however has provided her with means to bear rule over his will. He governs by law, fhe by perfuafion. Nor can her influence ever fail, if fupported by fweetnefs of temper and zeal to make him happy. Rousseau says charmingly, " Hers is a "sovereignty founded on complaisance " and address: caresses are her orders, " tears are her menaces. She governs in " the family as a minister does in the state, " procuring commands to be laid on her, " for doing what she inclines to do."

ALL beings are fitted by nature for their station. Domestic concerns are the province of the wife; and nature prompts young women to qualify themselves for behaving well in that station: young men never think of it. I know several ladies of good understanding, who, at the distance of weeks, can recal to memory the particulars of every dinner they had been invited to.

FROM a married woman engaged in family concerns, a more staid behaviour is expected, than from a young woman before

before marriage; and confequently, a greater fimplicity of drefs. Cornelia, daughter of the great Scipio, and mother of the Gracchi, makes a figure in the Roman ftory. She was vifited by a lady of rank, who valued drefs, and was remarked for an elegant toilet. Obferving every thing plain in Cornelia's apartment, "Madam, fays fhe, I wifh to fee "your toilet, for it muft be fuperb." Cornelia waved the fubject till her children came from fchool. "Thefe, my "good friend, are my ornaments, and "all I have for a toilet." Here is difplayed pure nature in perfection. A girl begins with her doll, then thinks of adorning her own perfon. When fhe is married, her children become her dolls, upon whom all her tafte in drefs is difplayed.

SECT.

SECT. IX.

INSTRUCTIONS *concerning the* CULTURE *of the* HEAD *or* UNDERSTANDING.

IN planning the present work, I had chiefly in view the culture of the heart; prompted by two motives, first, its superior importance in the conduct of life; next, its being in a great measure overlooked by writers upon education. The culture of the understanding has been so amply displayed by excellent writers, as to afford little matter for additions. As however there is a certain period, during which the culture of the head may be carried on jointly with that of the heart, the following hints are added relative to the former, and preparatory to a more regular course of instruction at school or college.

1*st*, IN order to smooth the road to knowledge, it ought to be a chief concern in the preceptor, to promote in his pupils an appetite for it. Give them examples of men, who, from a low state, have by learning arrived to great fame and honour. Let such examples be introduced occasionally, as a subject only of conversation. Leave the application to the young men; which will have a much finer effect, than if the preceptor himself should make the application.

2*d*, Boys ought so far to be treated like men, as to be informed before hand of the benefit expected from what they are ordered to do or to learn; which will make them apply with double vigour. Rousseau gives a lively example. His *Eleve*, before he could read, got a written invitation to a milk feast. He applied to every person in the family, desiring to know the contents of the billet; but they could not read, or pretended they could not. The opportunity was lost; and from that

that moment he was reftlefs till he was taught to read.

3*d*, In teaching children any art, reading for example, arithmetic, geography, let it not be confidered as a formal ftudy, but as an amufement. Cut letters in wood, give them names, fcatter them, and defire your *Eleve* to bring a particular letter. Let him try to imitate the letter that is brought. Employ him to count the number of panes in a window, or of fhillings on a table. Thefe hints may be varied a thoufand ways, much to his inftruction as well as amufement. An agreeable way of learning geography, is to have every county or kingdom by itfelf pafted on wood. After ftudying the general map, let your pupil try to join the parts into one whole. A pack of cards containing the names and pictures of great men, with a fhort account of them, will be an agreeable introduction to hiftory.

itory. Cards may be fuccefsfully applied to many other purpofes.

4th, It will facilitate the acquiring of any art, to divide it into all its diftinct branches. Before a child is taught to read, acquaint it with letters, next with fyllables, and then with words. Familiarize your pupil with the Greek letters, fo as to read Greek before you enter him upon the meaning. Begin not to teach Euclid, till he is well acquainted with the different figures. In that view, employ him to infcribe a circle in a fquare, a triangle in a circle, and fo on. This manual operation will be an enticing amufement: and at the fame time contribute to make the demonftrations more readily apprehended. Introduce him to the knowledge of the terreftrial globe, fo as to be able to point out every kingdom and every city, before commencing a regular courfe of geography.

5th, A CONTINUAL attention to a single object, is the hardest task that can be imposed on children. They are prone to variety, which is peculiarly useful in childhood, intended by nature for acquiring ideas. When the thoughts of a child begin to wander, change the subject. Rebuke and correction, commonly employed to force attention, fill the mind with fear and concern, leaving no room for other impressions.

6th, EXERCISE your children to recite stories they have heard or read. It improves their articulation, gives them words at command, and tends to form their stile. This ought to be a frequent occupation.

7th, WHEN the faculty of reason begins to make some figure, exercise your pupils to draw morals from fables well chosen. Present to them first fables of which the moral

moral is obvious and striking. Proceed to fables the moral of which is less obvious. The progress ought to be slow; for to draw a proper moral, requires much practice, or uncommon penetration. To facilitate that exercise, I recommend a little book entitled, *An Introduction to the Art of Thinking*. Take a hint also from the same book, to exercise your pupils in conjecturing the existence of unknown facts, from facts that are known. Take the following instance. Rousseau, in his travels through England, observing a smooth foot-path at the side of every high road, conjectures that the English must be highly benevolent, because they provide comfortable roads for the low people, who are neglected in every other country.

8*th*, To form a stile in young persons of twelve or thirteen, I suggest the following method. Take a long sentence in an English author, Lord Bolinbroke, for instance, who delights in long sentences; reduce it to the simplest arrangement, but so as to be perfectly intelligible. Employ your pupil to arrange it in the best order he can. After frequent trials with the tutor's observations on them, I have known much facility acquired in arrangement; sentences sometimes arranged, perhaps better than by the author himself.

9th, REGULAR hours at school of reading and of diversion, have a woful effect. Children, after a painful lesson, are let out to play. Their time, being circumscribed, appears always too short. From the height of amusement, they are forced back to a dry lesson. Can it be expected, that in such a state of mind they will listen to serious instruction? Let them play, let them fatigue themselves: guard only against sauntering. When sufficiently

ently tired, lead them back with a chearful countenance to a leſſon, as a change of amuſement. This is agreeable to human nature; and I hold it to be deciſive againſt a public ſchool, till young perſons have acquired as much underſtanding, as to be convinced of the benefit of inſtruction, without needing any collateral incitement. To torment young creatures with Latin before that time, is likely to make them abhor it. " Id in primis ca-
" vere opportebit, ne ſtudia, qui amare
" nondum poterit, oderit, et amaritudi-
" nem ſemel perceptam etiam ultra rudes
" annos reformidet *."

10*th*, The inſtructions given above, which can only be put in practice by a private tutor, ſhew the benefit, or rather neceſſity, of prolonging domeſtic education. There is another reaſon ſtill more cogent. A public ſchool anſwers finely
for

---

* Quintil. L. 1. C. 1.

for initiating young men in the manners of the world, leading each to mind himself, and to guard againſt others. But is there to be found in a public ſchool, a cenſor of manners, or a guardian of morals? The maſter concerns himſelf with neither, except that his diſciples behave orderly when he is lecturing. Nor indeed is it poſſible, that he can have conſtantly under his eye, ſuch numbers as are commonly at a public ſchool. Hence it is in a meaſure eſſential, that a young man be well tutored in morals, at leaſt, before he be left to himſelf, among a number of young men of very different diſpoſitions. Virtue, decency, order, conſiſt moſtly in reſtraint, a negative which makes no figure externally. It is the bold ſpirit, diſdaining reſtraint, that makes a figure, is admired and followed. Do parents apprehend no danger of their ſon being led aſtray at a public ſchool? Surely there is great danger, if he be not ſufficiently

ficiently prepared at home to refift temptation. In the Spectator, a young man is defcribed, who funk into vice by not being able to pronounce the monofyllable No. If you put any value on morals, permit not your fon to enter a public fchool, till he can pronounce with a manly affurance the monofyllable No.

11*th*, EPISTLES to friends, or to favourites, may be an amufement at a public fchool as well as at home; and this amufement may be encouraged as early as young folks have learned to write tolerably. It is an agreeable amufement: it improves their hand, and enures them to exprefs their thoughts readily. When they have learned the art of arranging fentences as above, the improvement it makes in their epiftles delights them.

12*th*, PEOPLE are induftrious to lay up a ftock of money for their children; but

few

few think of a more useful stock, that of ideas, though it can be procured in less time and with less labour. One who in youth has collected such a stock, who delights in reading, and who has acquired a habit of thinking and observing, can never pine for want of company. This person possesses the magic art of raising the dead, and conversing familiarly with the greatest men of past times. That source of entertainment never dries up, not even in old age. It is my sincere opinion, that a common peasant enjoys more felicity, than a man of fortune whose education has been neglected, who is so ignorant as even to put no value on knowledge, who lives from hour to hour without plan or prospect. It requires an extraordinary genius to lead an idle life with any degree of satisfaction or esteem. Company is not always in our power; and in company a man makes but a silly figure, however plentiful his board is, if he has nothing

nothing to say to his guests. I have in my eye a married couple, who began with a large stock of money; but no ideas except what were picked up occasionally, and consequently of the simplest kind. The sum of the man's learning was a smattering in Latin; and of the woman's, Dryden's plays, and two or three French romances. With that stock, scanty as it was, they made a tolerable shift the first years of their union. In youth the world is new; and a flow of spirits is in itself enjoyment. The couple are now old, in easy circumstances, but no fund of conversation, no taste for books, nothing to do. Is it not a deplorable case, to be as it were on the brink of happiness, and yet entirely excluded from it? The picture of sauntering Jack and idle Joan, has a foundation in nature.

13*th*, WITH respect to things proper to be known by persons of condition, I recommend

commend botany as a favourite, not what is commonly taught, fit only for those who intend to be profeſſors, but the powers and properties of plants, their flowers, their fruit, their odour, their cultivation, and in ſhort every particular that gives ſatisfaction to a reflecting mind. Married women of condition, cannot be more agreeably employed, than in adorning their gardens and pleaſure grounds with trees, ſhrubs and flowers, which bounteous nature produces in great variety for our amuſement. In this country, it is common to teach girls the harpſichord, which ſhows a pretty hand and a nimble finger, without ever thinking whether they have a genius for muſic, or even an ear. It ſerves indeed to fill a gap in time, which ſome parents are at a loſs how otherwiſe to employ. By all means, let their taſte in muſic be improved, if they have any, as well as in painting, and in the other fine arts; but I find no good reaſon for degrading young

young women of condition, to be muficians more than painters. Such laborious occupations, which confume much time, are proper for thofe only who purpofe to live by them. If, however, a young woman of rank, be violently bent on mufic or painting, it would be cruel to reftrain her; but I would yield with reluctance. I am not of the fame opinion with refpect to dancing. To be a good player on the harpfichord, requires only a fine ear with perfeverance: it is no index of mental faculties. To dance well, that is, to dance with grace and expreffion, a certain dignity of mind is requifite, fupported by good fenfe; and therefore, dancing well is an index of the mind. I add, that elegant motions in dancing, are communicated to walking and to every gefture. Much time, however, in teaching a girl to dance, is thrown away if fhe have not a pregnant genius: it is fufficient that her motions be made eafy, to prevent being aukward.

14*th*, As in forming the two sexes, every thing that tends to rivalship is avoided, nature ought to be copied in education. You cannot exceed in displaying to young women human nature, its principles, its passions, its faculties, its frailties; for by that branch of knowledge, their conduct is directed. History also ought to be their study as well as that of young men. A general knowledge of the sciences and of their utility, may be opened to them historically; because it will enable them to put a just value on men of learning, and withdraw them from fops and friblers. But avoid the intricacies of philosophy and deep reasoning; which would tend to emulation, not to cordiality. A woman of sense prudently educated, makes a delicious companion to a man of parts and knowledge. An ignorant woman, if she consult her peace of mind, will accept of no man for a husband, but who is ignorant like herself. She cannot be be a companion for a man of knowledge; and the sense of her inferiority renders her unhappy. To people who labour for bread, conversation is very little necessary, but essential to persons of rank; and therefore, to unite in matrimony, a man of taste and knowledge, with a shallow female, is indeed woful. What figure will such a woman make in educating their offspring; and how mortifying must it be to the man to have his children ill educated? How can she train them to virtue when she is ignorant of the means? She knows of no means but flattery or threats, which, far from improving, render them insolent or timid.

15*th*, It is curious to observe the progress of nature in bestowing knowledge. Children learn words before they can speak; and when they can speak, they employ these words to explain what they want,

want, obscurely indeed for some time. The full import of words being learned by degrees, children express themselves more and more accurately, as they advance toward maturity. There are however many words which are never perfectly understood by the generality, *personal identity* for example, *chance, space. Taste* is a common word; and yet it would puzzle many a good writer, to give it a precise meaning. Were teachers reduced to use no word but what their pupils perfectly understand, instruction could not begin before maturity of age; and much later, if ever, with many. Yet the celebrated Rousseau, overlooking the progress of nature, maintains strenuously, that in teaching children, no word ought to be used but what denotes something they are acquainted with, that is, some known object of the external senses. With respect to the fable of the fox and raven, he pronounces it absurd

to

to mention these animals to a child, if it has never seen them. I cannot subscribe to this opinion. A child may know that a raven is a bird, and a fox a beast, without having seen either. With that imperfect knowledge, however, the child may understand the fable as well as if it had seen both. People of Europe talk familiarly of a lion, and with intelligence; though few in that part of the world ever saw a lion. With respect to geography, he observes, that to point out countries and towns in a map, is but an imperfect way of teaching their true position. I grant; and would take a better way if it were in my offer. Teaching, however, by the map is far from being useless: the pupil retains the position of places as delineated there; and when his faculties ripen, he readily transfers that ideal position from the map to the globe of the earth. Rousseau declares against teaching history, till young people

people are ripe for judging of caufes and confequences. This, with many, would prove a very late beginning. I am for teaching hiftory as foon as the plain facts can be comprehended; *firſt*, becaufe it is agreeable to children; and *next*, becaufe it makes the facts known and ready for ufe when people are able to judge of caufes and confequences. At that rate, a child fhould never hear the name of God. That word fignifies a Being, of whom the moſt penetrating philofopher has but an obfcure conception, which muft be ftill more obfcure in a child. It is proper however, to give children an impreffion of a good Being, who made us and protects us. Their notion of a Deity, will purify as they grow up.

16*th*, So far indeed I heartily agree with Rouffeau, that in teaching children, the fimpleft words fhould be preferred, where it can be done. This concludes ftill more

forcibly

forcibly against employing general rules; for they are above the comprehension of children; instruction goes on better and more pleasantly without them. In teaching a language, it is the universal practice to begin with grammar, and to do every thing by rule. I affirm this to be a most preposterous method. Grammar is contrived for men, not for children. Its natural place is between language and logic: it ought to close lectures on the former, and to be the first lectures on the latter. It is a gross deception that a language cannot be taught without rules. A boy who is flogged into grammar-rules, makes a shift to apply them; but he applies them by rote, like a parrot. Boys, for the knowledge they acquire of a language, are not indebted to dry rules, but to practice and observation. To this day, I never think without shuddering of Difputer's grammar, which was my daily persecution during the most important period

period of life. Curiosity, when I was farther advanced in years, prompted me to look into a book that had given me so much trouble. At this time, I understood the rules perfectly; and was astonished that formerly they had been to me words without meaning, which I had been taught to apply mechanically, without knowing how or why. Deplorable it is, that young creatures should be so punished without being guilty of any fault—more than sufficient to produce a disgust at learning, instead of promoting it. Whence then the absurdity of persecuting boys with grammar-rules? Pride is the cause. By using rules, the teacher of Latin flatters himself, that his profession equals in dignity that of logic and mathematics, to which rules are essential. Even a humble teacher of English to children four or five years old, will, in spite of common sense, make a figure by his rules.

SECT.

SECT. X.

Short Essays *on particular Subjects relative to the* Culture *of the* Heart.

ART. I.

Selfishness *and* Benevolence *compared.*

THE restlessness of man has been a topic of frequent declamation; " That after much thought and labour " in the pursuit of any good, the acqui- " sition bestows but a momentary plea- " sure; that the person becomes as rest- " less as before, in the pursuit of some " new object; and in short, that most " men pass life in toil and anxiety, with- " out ever resting contented with what " they possess." Writers who have a just sense of religion, account for this disposition from the following principle, " That

"That this life is to us a time of trial, to prepare for a better; and that happiness in it, beside being inconsistent with such a trial, would divert our thoughts from a better life." Other writers who have no thought but of our present state, hold this disposition to be a gross imperfection in human beings, made as it would appear not for their own happiness, but for some latent purpose.

As the tracing the ways of Providence has always been to me a favourite study, I chearfully enter the lists against the writers last mentioned.

There may be animals which have no enjoyment beyond rest and food. But man is not so made. His constitution fits him for action; and he takes pleasure in it. Did he take delight in rest, he would be an absurd being, considering

ing that this earth produces little for him but what requires preparation; that raw materials are furnished in plenty, but that much labour is requisite to convert them into food, cloathing, habitation. I observe further, that though the feeds of all valuable knowledge are born with us, yet that persevering culture is necessary to make them productive. What then would man be in his present state, were rest his delight, his *summum bonum?*

Thus, upon the activity of man, depend all his comforts internal and external. "Admitted, say my antagonists. "Man is not blamed for his activity in "procuring the comforts of life; but "for his restlessness in never being sa- "tisfied with his present comforts." These writers certainly will not condemn restlessness in the lump: they will approve restlessness in doing good; which undoubtedly is one of the noblest properties

perties that belong to human nature. Restlessness then, as far as reprehensible, must be confined to the selfish passions. Nor can all of these be comprehended; for surely there is no vice in restlessness to acquire fame, or the good will of others. Restlessness with regard to corporeal enjoyments, I acknowledge to be hurtful. Nor is it even there a defect in the nature of man, but one of the pernicious consequences of indulging such enjoyments to excess. As they are the lowest enjoyments of our nature, intemperance in them soon produces satiety and disgust; from which the luxurious have no relief but by frequent change of objects. This miserable restlessness, the fruit of intemperance in grovelling pleasures, will not find a single votary. Consider on the other hand a social disposition. A man of benevolence, whose happiness chiefly consists in serving others, can never rest satisfied in his present

sent state: opportunities of doing good daily occur, and employ him without end. The more opulent he is, the more restless he will be; because opulence multiplies his opportunities of doing good.

Activity is essential to a social being: to a selfish being it is of no use, after procuring the means of living. A selfish man, who by his opulence has all the luxuries of life at command, and dependents without number, has no occasion for activity. Hence it may fairly be inferred, that were man destined by Providence to be entirely selfish, he would be disposed by his constitution to rest, and never would be active when he could avoid it. The natural activity of man therefore, is to me evidence, that his Maker did not intend him to be purely a selfish being.

This

This leads me to compare selfishness with benevolence. Selfishness in one instance is not only innocent but laudable, which is in coveting fame or good will. These appetites however prevail but in few, compared with the appetite for corporeal pleasures. It would be too extensive for the present essay, to show all the advantages of benevolence over corporeal pleasures; that no corporeal pleasure contributes so much to happiness as the exercise of benevolence; that the latter raises a man in his own esteem, and in that of others, whereas the former lessens him in both. I shall therefore confine myself to one particular, which is the superior advantage of benevolence from its permanency. Corporeal pleasures, however sweet at first, soon lose their relish; nor is there any way to prevent satiety, but change of objects. This is strongly exemplified in that low commerce between the sexes, founded on the carnal appetite

appetite merely; which requires new objects daily, becaufe the fame object foon difgufts. Nor can novelty long fupport this grovelling appetite: frequent repetition without waiting the calls of nature, blunts the charm of novelty: every new object appears lefs and lefs new; and that charm vanifhes long before middle age. This fuggefts a fecond inference, that were man intended to be entirely a felfifh being, his life would be made much fhorter than it is. Benevolence on the contrary acquires vigour by exercife, and the more good we do, the more we are inclined to do. The fatisfaction it affords is not blunted even by old age, which blunts every other enjoyment. The body may decay, but the pleafure of doing good, when habitual, continues the fame, even to the laft moment of exiftence *.

LISTE.

* With refpect to thofe who are in conftant purfuit of pleafure, which as conftantly efcapes their grafp,

LISTEN to this doctrine ye parents and tutors: and haften to infpire thofe under your care with affection to their fellow creatures. Let them know, that, even for their own fake, benevolence is greatly preferable to felfifhnefs. This leffon, it is true, may be gathered in the commerce of the world; but if the mind be left without inftruction, it is apt to acquire a felfifh bias; and then the leffon comes too late. Teach your pupils fubmiffion to fuperiors, and civility and complaifance to inferiors. Let acts of benevolence be their daily exercife. Give them money for charity, and accuftom them to account how it has been laid out. Let them

---

a writer of fpirit exclaims as follows. "At that rate "poverty is the greateft bleffing of life. By delay-"ing gratification of the appetites, it makes gratifica-"tion a pleafure. It keeps the foul awake with ex-"pectation, and enlivens it with hope. In a word, "the reputed wretch, who begs from door to door, "is really happier than the rich man who has every "pleafure in his power; and yet, from the eafinefs "of attainment, feels no gratification."

them visit the sick, and carry to them what is proper for their relief. Exhort them to be kindly to their companions, and to be ready to assist them in distress. Convince them, that in such conduct they will find much more gratification, than in yielding to selfish appetites. Benevolence thus cultivated in children, becomes, in time, their ruling passion: they will be the delight of their parents, a blessing to their relations, and the objects of universal good will and esteem.

ART. II.

Opinion and Belief less influenced by Reason than by Temper and Education.

IN the reign of Tiberius Cæsar, Severus Cæcina insisted to have it enacted, that no Roman governor should carry his wife with him to his province. He said, " that he had a wife and six children, " and

" and that he always left them at home,
" though, in different provinces, he had
" borne arms for the republic more than
" forty years; that by such attendants
" peace degenerates into luxury, war in-
" to confusion, and a Roman army into
" a mob of barbarians; that not only
" weak and unequal to labour is the fe-
" male sex, but, where not restrained,
" cruel and greedy of power: that they
" love to range among the soldiers, and
" to cabal with the leaders." He intreated the senate to consider the dangerous tendency of bribery and corruption
in a governor. " Yet how often, added
" he, have their wives been noted for
" these crimes! The infamous of every
" province cling to them for refuge;
" which establishes in effect two gover-
" nors in a province, and opposite in-
" terests. The paying court to the wives
" of magistrates, prohibited by our old
" laws, seems now to be in oblivion; and
" these

"these ladies, not satisfied to domineer
"at home, infest the courts of justice,
"armies, and the senate." Cœcina ended without applause: a confused murmur
spread through the assembly. Valerius
Messalinus answered thus. "Our fore-
"fathers, involved in perpetual war, and
"reduced frequently to defend the gates
"of Rome, were rigid in discipline, and
"austere in manners. We have now
"no enemy to fear: victorious Rome is
"the seat of empire. Peaceable times
"produce kindly manners; and our old
"customs have yielded to gentleness and
"humanity. Society between husband
"and wife is founded on nature; and
"nature ought to prevail. Against the
"enemy let us march with nothing but
"our arms: returning victorious, why
"should we be denied the reward of a
"comfortable companion? Some women
"are prone to avarice or ambition; and
"so are some men. Is the latter a good
"reason

" reason for leaving our provinces with-
" out governors? Some men have been
" corrupted by their wives; but are all
" bachelors of unspotted fame? Because
" of a few instances of bad women, shall
" our citizens be deprived of their great-
" est blessing, in adversity as well as in
" prosperity? In vain do we lay our
" vices upon others: let us fairly ac-
" knowledge the fault to be in the hus-
" band, when the wife goes astray. Is
" it of no moment, that by the projected
" law the brittle sex would be exposed to
" their own luxury, and to the lust of
" profligate men? As the husband's pre-
" sence is no more than sufficient to keep
" his wife within bounds, ought a law
" to be made for separating them? Thus
" in straining for a remedy to foreign
" evils, we open a door to unbounded
" vice at home." Drusus the Emperor's
adopted son added, " That princes are
" often called to distant expeditions:
" how

"how often did Augustus visit the extremities of his empire, accompanied with his faithful Livia! That he himself has led armies far from the city, and was ready at all times to serve his country; but would go with little satisfaction, if torn from his dear wife, the worthy mother of many children." I need not inform the reader that Tacitus is my author, who adds, that the motion was rejected.

To which side does the reader incline? This question is, in appearance, deeply political; and yet I violently suspect, that the good of the state was not what moved any of the speakers. Imagine a grave senator with a long beard, standing up and delivering what follows: "Gentlemen, each of you have in your own opinion, urged unanswerable arguments; and is surprised, that any should stand out against conviction.

"But

" But I let you into a secret, that your
" arguments have not convinced even
" yourselves. Your conviction is found-
" ed upon character, not in the least
" upon reasons of state. You Drusus are
" in the flower of youth, vigorous, and
" delighting in the commerce of women.
" —You Cœcina are old, crabbed, and
" long past the pleasures of youth."

It is an observation universally admitted, that in the conduct of life, men are influenced more by passion and prejudice than by reason. A man who is prone to suspicion and distrust, will be jealous of his wife, and lock up every thing from his servants. One addicted to society, has no existence but in a crowd. A person on the contrary of a solitary disposition, retires to the mountains, and declares war against the feathered kind. " Is it not more innocent,
" says he, to make war upon birds than
" upon

" upon men?" The man must be wondrous cool who is always obsequious to reason: he would indeed be a singular phænomenon. Is there any thing more common than a person going astray, notwithstanding the admonitions of conscience? Passion, it is true, does not always appear so openly. It frequently by deep disguise convinces us, that our opinions and belief are founded on solid principles. Thus, being imposed on by passion under the mask of reason, self-deceit is spread through the human race. The story above mentioned, is a noted instance; and such occur every day. Show me a man who is fired with ambition and love of power: you, in vain, will attempt to convince him, that Alexander was not a greater man than Socrates. The opinions we form of men and things, are the result of affection more than of evidence. An advice given by a man of figure, is highly regarded:

the same advice from one in low condition, is despised or neglected. A courageous person under-rates danger: to the indolent the slightest obstacle appears unsurmountable. A person of veracity, relying on the veracity of others, is easy of belief: where a man's veracity is so supple as to bend to his interest, he will be suspicious of evidence and hard of belief. Hence it is, that upon the benevolent and humane, the arguments for the goodness of the Deity, make a deeper impression, than on the sullen and morose. How important then is the art of education, when upon it in a great measure depend, not only our behaviour and conduct; but even our judgment and understanding, by which chiefly we are elevated above the brute creation! What can be more interesting to human beings, than their conviction of the existence of a benevolent Deity, their Maker, their Father, their Protector? Did parents seriously

ously consider, that this conviction depends in some measure upon our disposition, they would neglect no opportunity of sweetning the temper of their children, and improving their benevolence. The time for such discipline, is confined to pupilage, when the mind, like wax, is deeply susceptible of impressions. At maturity, it becomes inflexible like the body, and then culture comes too late. Against passions and prejudices that never have been controlled, the most cogent reasons signify little. Arguments that accord with a man's taste are greedily swallowed, while the unpalatable are rejected with disgust. He is therefore no adept in logic, who hopes to convince others by arguments that have weight with himself. He ought to study the temper of the person he would convince, and urge the arguments that are suited to that temper. Drusus was fond of glory; and Cæcina might have prevailed,

vailed, had he painted in lively colours, how glorious it would be to sacrifice private pleasures to the service of the state. But to urge that women are vicious creatures, was not likely to make an impression on Drusus, who thought that all women were honest because his wife was an angel.

SEEING then that our opinions and belief depend greatly on passion and prepossession, little upon reason, and not at all upon will, how extravagant is the attempt to force conviction by rewards and punishments! Suppose that the law had taken place prohibiting governors of provinces to carry their wives along with them; and that the Emperor had ordered all the world to be of his opinion, under a grievous penalty. The order probably would have produced plenty of dissemblers, but not a single convert. To make me believe under the terror of punishment,

nishment, that the earth rests upon a huge elephant, or that an eclipse presages some dire calamity, is no less absurd than an endeavour to force a dwarf to be six feet high, or a negro to have a white complexion. What then shall be thought of persecution for difference of opinion in points of faith? Often in perusing histories of persecution, I have started up as from sleep, and imagined that all the while I had been dreaming. And yet in fact that monster Persecution, the offspring of wild bigotry, has shed more blood than the fiercest wars for power and glory. Considering that to believe is not in our power, more than to be hot or cold, would one imagine it possible, that, by misguided education, a rational being can be made to believe the most palpable absurdities, as that bread and wine, in direct contradiction to our senses, are flesh and blood; or that an old frail man becomes infallible, the moment he

is

is elected a bishop, with a triple crown on his head; or that gross inconsistencies affirmed in the creed of St Athanasius, must be believed under the pain of eternal damnation*. Such examples of perverse education, tending to enervate the faculty of reason, and to make us blindly submissive to the crafty and designing, ought to call forth the most fervent zeal of parents to have their children properly educated. It is not sufficient that they are taught morality and the rules of conduct: their rational powers ought to be exercised and fortified, in order to judge what they ought to believe, and what they ought not to believe. What a heavy charge then lies against those parents, who, instead of instructing their children in

---

* What are we to think of those men who introduced that infernal creed into the Liturgy of the Church of England; and consequently joined with the author in devoting to eternal flames every person Jew or Gentile, Turk or Christian, who does not faithfully believe every absurdity it contains.

in the principles of reason, the noblest faculty of man, leave them open to every wrong impression that may be stamped on the tender mind, by chance, or by the depravity of people about them!

ART. III.

DIFFERENCES in OPINION make the Cement of SOCIETY.

IT appears to me the utmost perversion of human nature, that people differing in opinion, even with respect to religion, cannot live peaceably together, not to say happily. Men join in society for mutual aid and support; and they submit to be governed, because government is essential to society. But how far does this submission extend? Surely not to a man's private thoughts and opinions: these he may indulge as his reason dictates to him.

The legiflature has no concern, provided he keep them to himfelf without difturbing fociety. Toleration is thus a dictate of common fenfe, and as fuch is now permitted every where. And yet, the civil war in France between the Catholics and Huguenots, was founded upon a doctrine directly contrary. The Huguenots pleaded for liberty of confcience: the Catholics, bitter enemies to it, infifted that none fhould be permitted to breathe the French air who differed from them in the flighteft punctilio. Perufing that hiftory, it often occurred to me as a horrid depravity of temper in human beings, to devote to deftruction one another for a caufe that gives no difturbance at prefent, and which ought never to have given difturbance. Yet even in France, perfecution raged contrary to the nature of the people; and brought that great monarchy to the brink of ruin. Would one believe, that by vicious education

men

men can be converted into monsters, worse than beasts of prey who spare their own kind * ?

This history suggested the following thoughts upon uniformity in point of opinion. Were it even practicable, by persecution or other means, to produce uniformity in opinion; the effect, far from being desirable, would be dismal. All nature is full of variety; and the mind of man corresponds to it, being prone to variety, and delighting in it. We feel as in fetters when long confined to one object: a blended scene of woods, rivers, plains, mountains, men walking, cattle grazing, a cottage here, a steeple there, gives more pleasure than the sky,

the

---

* It is mentioned by Sully in his Memoirs, that on a visit to Madame de Maltin his aunt, she received him very coldly, saying she had disinherited him, because he neither believed in God nor in his saints, and worshipped none but the devil. This was the notion her father confessor had given her of all Protestants.

the ocean, or any other single object, however grand. To a well disposed mind it must be equally entertaining, to look down, as it were from an eminence, upon the various tempers, sentiments, opinions, and pursuits of human beings, tending to different ends, clashing indeed and interfering, but upon the whole conspiring to the general good. " Endless
" differences in temper, in taste, and in
" mental faculties, that of reason in par-
" ticular, produce necessarily variety in
" sentiment and in opinion. Can God
" be displeased with such variety, when
" it is his own work? He requires no
" uniformity except with respect to an
" upright mind and clear conscience,
" which are indispensable. Here opens
" at the same time an illustrious final
" cause. Different features and different
" expressions of countenance in the hu-
" man race, not only distinguish one
" person from another, but promote so-
                                    " ciety,

"ciety, by aiding us to chuse a friend,
"an associate, a partner for life. Differ-
"ences in opinion and sentiment, have
"effects still more beneficial: they rouse
"the attention, give exercise to the un-
"derstanding, and sharpen the reason-
"ing faculty. With respect to religion
"in particular, perfect uniformity, which
"furnishes no subject for thinking nor
"for reasoning, would produce languor
"in divine worship, and make us sink
"into cold indifference *." Is this a doctrine that will justify the oceans of Christian blood that have been shed in support of it? Saladin, one of the greatest men that ever existed, had, even in the dark age of superstition and bigotry, very different notions. It is reported of him, that in his latter-will, he ordered large sums to be distributed among the poor, without any distinction of Mahometans,

* Sketches of the History of Man, Edit. 2. Vol. 4. p. 477.

tans, Jews, or Christians; willing to have it understood, that all men are brethren, and that charity ought not to consider what men believe, but what they suffer.

But as the absurdity of expecting uniformity in point of religion stands now manifest to all the world, I shall confine my speculation to a more mild subject, that will raise no indignation nor bad humour. I begin with asking this simple question, What comfort would society afford, and conversation one of its chief supports, without variety in humour and sentiment? Language would be useless, and no uniting tie would remain but of many hands to procure the necessities of animal life. Man would degenerate into a brute—an illustrious effect, worthy to be enforced by fire and sword! Is this to copy nature, which diversifies our minds as much as our faces? What then shall be thought of those who in company

pany are rude to every one who differs from them? Is such behaviour more excusable than to pull every one by the nose whose face displeases them? I cannot illustrate this topic more agreeably than by a fable from a French author, which I venture to put into the English dress. "Four friends there were, linked in
"close union. If they differed, it might
"be in sentiment, but never in affection.
"One was for the fair beauty, another for
"the brown: one dealt in prose, another
"relished verse. Frequent were their de-
"bates, but all tending to enliven con-
"versation. One day, a favourite topic
"was brought upon the carpet. They
"took sides, grew keen, their blood was
"up, nothing but noise instead of reason.
"They parted in bad humour, scarce sen-
"sible of friendship to one another. After
"having time to cool, Gentlemen, says
"one of them, how happy for friends to
"be always of one mind: let us humbly
"pray

"pray the gods for that blſſing. No
"ſooner ſaid than done. They marched
"in a body to the temple of Apollo, and
"preſented their ſupplication. The god
"inclining his ear, granted their re-
"queſt; and in the twinkling of an eye,
"they were perfectly uniſon. One made
"an obſervation; all concurred. One
"declared his opinion; the reſt gave a
"nod. Good, ſaid they! Farewel dif-
"putes, we wiſh them a good journey.
"But behold: the charm of ſociety has
"journeyed with them. No more amu-
"ſing converſations, no beautiful reflec-
"tions, no ſhining thoughts, ſtruck out
"by oppoſition, that enlighten the mind
"and chear the heart—Aye, is now the
"only word. Friendſhip ſubſided, indif-
"ference encroached, and irkſome grew
"the hours that formerly glided ſweetly
"along. Entire concord diſſolved the
"union. Let men forbear mending the
"works of nature: we are well enough

"as we are. Give all men the same turn of mind, and you take away the very salt of society. UNIFORMITY brought forth: to her infant she gave the name of DISGUST."

SPECULATIONS like the present, have a tendency to banish bigotry in opinion. There are indeed certain opinions that ought to be universal, because they are grafted on our nature. I would persecute every opinion contradictory to the following propositions, that there is a Deity to whom we owe gratitude and worship; and that there is a right and a wrong in actions, which ought to regulate the conduct of every human being. But I would persecute the opinions only, not the persons who hold them: they are the objects of pity, not of persecution. It is not in the power of man to eradicate his opinions, more than his feelings or his appetites. How absurd then is it

to

to punish a man for what he cannot help? There is not in science a principle more evident than that now mentioned, which every man must assent to when fairly stated. Yet such is the influence of passion and prejudice, as to have rendered that principle invisible for many ages. What rancour, distress, and bloodshed would have been prevented even among Christians, had the absurdity of persecution been displayed to them in open day light? This doctrine ought to be carefully instilled into young minds, hitherto free from bias. Let it be inculcated early into both sexes, that men are not accountable for their opinions, more than for their faces; and that a wry opinion, even in matters of religion, is not the subject of punishment, more than a wry shape. I include opinions however slightly founded, provided only they be sincere and agreeable to conscience. It is indeed a sort of Herculean labour, to eradicate notions that

that from infancy have been held fundamental. But the mind of a child is white paper, ready to receive any impreſſion, good or bad. This is the precious time for impreſſions, though too early for regular inſtruction. Let it not be trifled away, for it never can be recalled. Good impreſſions ſtamped on the mind at that early age, ſink deep and never are obliterated. Therefore, neglect no opportunity of ſetting virtue and vice before your child, in their proper colours: repeat to it often, that if it be good, every perſon will love it; if naughty, that every perſon will hate it; and, in a word, that happineſs is the reſult of virtue; miſery of vice. Give me the naming of the tutor, and the pupil ſhall partake of the angelic nature, or of the nature of a beaſt of prey.

I finiſh with obſerving hiſtorically, that the art of Printing, among its other advantages,

advantages, has had an influence to eradicate persecution, by spreading every where knowledge and rational principles. Even those who are the most prone to persecution, begin to hesitate. Reason, resuming her sovereign authority, will banish it altogether. It is true, that no farther back than the beginning of the present century, Mr Locke, even by Protestants, was held grossly heterodox for maintaining toleration. I am however hopeful, that within the next century it will be thought strange, that persecution should have prevailed among social beings. It will perhaps even be doubted, whether it ever was seriously put in practice.

ART. IV.

PARTIALITY.

AN officer of the revenue, rich by oppression, had a son and a servant intimate companions. They would pass the live-long day in conversing about masters and fathers. " Masters now-a-
" days are mere Turks, says Martin the
" valet, no regard for us; labour into-
" lerable, threatnings, blows; but of
" wages, not a word. Do they take us
" for unbaptized beasts of burden? All
" true, says the son; but, my dear Mar-
" tin, are fathers less hard hearted? In-
" cessant chiding, vexatious admoniti-
" ons, tedious lectures. Can the fools ex-
" pect we should have all the dull gravity
" of old age? Does a young man incline
" to the army? he is condemned to the
" long robe. Crossed he must be in every
" inclination, as if the old dotard were

"to chuse for him, not he for himself.
"No! adds he, there is not a race of men
"more intolerable than fathers." This
was their constant theme. Martin, employed in the finances, succeeded, became a tax-gatherer, had a sumptuous house, a luxurious table, a grand equipage, and a nation of valets. The son improved his father's stock, took a wife, and had children. Martin, now rich, became a reputable companion. They continued good friends. But what was now their theme? Why, children and servants. "O the cross of domestics, says Monsieur
"Martiniere, (for Martin's name was
"now extended a full span), thoughtless
"and lazy; threats and blows are in
"vain,—thieves, traitors, liars, they eat
"our bread and laugh at us to the bar-
"gain. Ah! says the father of the fa-
"mily, talk to me of children, there's
"the real cross, good for nothing boy or
"girl, no obedience.—We fatigue our-
"selves

" felves to death for them; but as to
" gratitude, your fervant. They long for
" our death, watch the inftant; and how
" happy when relieved of a burden."

A MAN is a partial judge in his own
caufe. Full of his imagined fuperiority,
he lofes fight of what he owes to others.
Fancying himfelf on a throne, to him all
muft bend the knee. A low man rails
at his fuperiors: he is exalted, lofes fight
of what he was, and now rails at himfelf in his former condition. The poor
never ceafe wondering at the narrow
views of the opulent, and at their want
of charity. Give them riches, their tone
varies; and now not a fyllable but of
the refpect due to people of their rank.
When fuch is the prepoffeffion even of
the loweft claffes, can a more fober way of
thinking be expected from thofe of high
birth? Kings naturally are not more depraved than other men; and but for

felf-self-partiality, it would be difficult to account why selfishness is their ruling passion; with scarce any sense of justice, far less of benevolence.

Self-partiality is the source of manifold distresses. A man infected with that disease, never thinks he is treated with sufficient respect: needs there more to imbitter his life, and to unfit him for society? peevishness and discontent render him miserable, in the very circumstances that make others happy. It was a problem among the ancient sages, why men commonly are so well satisfied with themselves, and so little with their condition. Had they thought of self-partiality, it would have solved the problem. A man of that temper never imagines that his condition equals his merit.

Self-partiality is difficult to be cured. It is a distemper that a man sees clearly in others, never in himself; and one will not readily submit to a cure who is not sensible of needing it. The great Cicero is a mortifying instance of this distemper. He was vain of his consulate, and exhorts his friend Lucceius, who was writing the history of Rome, to bestow the utmost energy of his pen in magnifying his exploits. " Make it," says he, " a splendid story ; for, in relating the " transactions of your friend, a deviation " from truth may well be excused." Did any man ever betray an appetite for fame more gross and unjustifiable ? Yet in several of his epistles to Brutus and to Cato, he declares that he was entirely free from vanity ; and that no other mortal had less regard to common fame and vulgar applause. A gentleman of a peevish temper, but to which self-partiality made him blind, had a small estate in the neighbourhood of a nobleman who delighted in hunting. If the chace led the hunters

into

into his fields, he was impatient and discontented, even without suffering any harm. One time, in the bitterness of wrath, he wrote to the Earl, that there could not be a greater curse than to be his neighbour. Urged by debt, he offered his estate to sale; and the Earl, to be rid of him, was glad to give the price demanded, much above the value. But change of residence did not change his temper. Every new neighbour appeared to him worse than all the former. "Strange!" exclaimed he, "that I can-
"not settle any where without finding a
"Lord H—." *Know thyself*, is a difficult lesson, especially for a young person who is not aware of self-partiality. The tutor ought to apply himself diligently to correct it in his pupil; assuring him, that of all vices it is the aptest to raise disgust. Bishop Butler in one of his admirable sermons, gives the following sagacious lesson: "Do not pretend," says he, "that your
"friend

"friend has any defects; but put him up-
"on thinking, what his enemies would say
"were they to attack his character. Let
"him beware of what he suspects they
"would mention as vicious or defective;
"not that he is to suppose them in the
"right, but that there may be some weak-
"ness there which he ought to guard
"against. This is the true way," adds
the good Bishop, " of making our ene-
"mies contribute to our good." If even
by such discipline self-partiality cannot
be totally eradicated, it may at least be
concealed. In weighing my own opinion against that of my opponent, what if I should rack my invention to discover what may be urged for him? Frequent practice may possibly abate my self-partiality. This lesson is with energy expressed in the following golden rule, " Do as you would be done by."

PARTIALITY,

PARTIALITY, checked or disguised, when entirely selfish, is allowed full scope when our country is the object, or our friend, or our religion *. This sort of partiality is laudable, if it provoke not our hatred against others. Excited by partiality to their country, the old Romans were flaming patriots. But their partiality was indulged to an ungenerous excess: they became proud, insolent, intolerable, holding all other nations as brutes and barbarians, the Greeks scarcely excepted. Such partiality is not unjust only, but inexcusable; being an infallible symptom of a mean understanding and of a contracted heart. It must be a bad frame

---

* A very sensible and religious woman, lately deceased, had a great friendship for David Hume the philosopher. When rallied on it, she insisted that he was the best christian of her acquaintance, that she read all his works as they were published, that to be sure there was a little philosophical nonsense in them; but still that he was a good christian. "For, added "she, have I not been intimately acquainted with "David Hume since he was a child."

frame of mind that sets us at variance with our fellow creatures, and foments discord instead of sweetning society.

But the bad effects of partiality in hurting others, are not to be compared with its bad effects in hurting ourselves. Every enmity we indulge, is to us a real misfortune: it so far imbitters our chief fund of happiness, which consists in benevolence and internal quiet. What then must he suffer, who hates every person who differs from him in sentiment. Such is the dismal condition of the bigot in religion, and factious man in the state, objects however of pity more than of aversion.

Benevolence, the most estimable of all principles, may, by a wrong direction of our passions, generate malevolence in abundance. If we be taught to confine our good will to our connections, and to hold others at defiance; the man who has from nature the greatest stock of benevolence, becomes by that wrong bias the most zealous clansman, and the most violent stickler for a party; which inflames his aversion to others in proportion. Thus the spirit of faction, opposition, and enmity, are by wrong education raised and fostered. Pictures of that kind are far from being rare. Reflect only on the state of this nation two centuries ago. The old Roman patriotism, which comprehended the whole Roman people, was among us confined to our tribe or clan. What inveteracy of one tribe against another! Worse than lions and tigers, which spare their own kind, we hunted one another down, and man became the most formidable enemy of man.

PEOPLE acquainted with their countrymen only, are apt to take up a prejudice against

against the manners and customs of other nations; which tends to narrow the spirit of benevolence, and to lessen their satisfaction in the society of their fellow creatures. Liberal education, and travelling with a view to instruction, are the only remedies. An incident recorded by Herodotus sets in a striking light the partiality of a nation to its own customs. Darius king of Persia, having an army composed of different nations, demanded of his Greek soldiers what bribe would prevail to make them eat the bodies of their dead parents, as the Indians did. It being answered, that nothing should ever tempt them to commit a crime so atrocious, the Prince in their presence demanded of some Indians, what sum would tempt them to burn the bodies of their parents after death. The Indians intreated the King to impose upon them any thing less horrible. That this was rank prejudice in the Indians, will be acknowledged

ledged by every European. But were the learned and polished Greeks free from that taint? We prefer the Greek manners and customs, which are familiar to us as their books make a capital branch of a learned education. The laying of a dead body on a funeral pile, appears to us as natural as the laying of it in earth. But let us figure an Egyptian, who, proud of his own country, never gave himself the trouble to think of foreign customs. Embalming was a sacred rite among that people, in order to preserve entire the bodies of their ancestors: the palaces of the dead were little less sumptuous than of the living. What notion would an Egyptian have of a people, whose practice he should be told it was, to throw their ancestors into the fire, or to let them rot in the earth? Yet the sentiment of the simple Indian was the same. Being ignorant of the art of embalming, the reverence he had for his parents,

prompted

prompted him to give them the most honourable grave in his power, which was, to convert them into his own substance. Brutality or savageness it could not be, when they expressed such horror at the Grecian mode. Their reverence indeed for their parents must have been excessive, when it was sufficient to overbalance the aversion that men, as well as other animals, have to feed on their own species.

If in this manner, young persons can be trained to examine with candour the manners and customs of different nations, they will find less reason than is commonly thought for preferring their own. Lead them to reflect that the manners and customs of nations, depend more on accident than on solid causes. The following is a ludicrous instance. A long beard is among us a mark of gravity, and commands respect; nor is it without reason that

that we imagine this to be a natural impreſſion. Yet in the reign of Francis I. of France, the grave judges of the parliament of Paris were obliged to be cloſe ſhaven. It was faſhionable among the courtiers and young beaux, to encourage the beard and to cut it into ſhapes. The beard accordingly was at that time a mark of levity, and therefore inconſiſtent with the ſolemn air of a judge.

As it is difficult to ſubdue partiality when it has once got a ſeat in the mind, parents and tutors ought to give peculiar attention, to preſerve thoſe under their care from the infection, noxious to themſelves, and noxious to others. Self-partiality is in particular the parent of opiniatrety; and young perſons cannot have a worſe guide, in their commerce with the world. Let them keep in mind, their frequent miſtakes and frequent change of ſentiment. Candour in acknowledging

ing error will gain them friends, more certainly than the mere negative of never having erred. Such candour will prevent many a blush and irksome reflection, which they are well acquainted with, who cannot bear ever to be thought in the wrong. A habit of ingenuity makes a man a comfortable companion, and fits him for every enjoyment of social life.

ART. V.

ASSOCIATION *of* IDEAS.

A MAN while awake is constantly thinking. Ideas pass in his mind without a gap or interval, forming a succession of related thoughts or ideas, following one another according to an established law of nature. Our external actions are in a great measure governed by this succession, there being an intimate connection

connection between thought and action. Did our thoughts flow on, without any mutual relation, and without any relation to our external actions; we should be hurried from thought to thought, and from action to action, entirely at the mercy of chance*. It is of importance in the education of youth, that this succession be preserved entire, free from ill-sorted ideas that have originally no relation. Any unlucky bias by which unrelated ideas are conceived to be related, is sufficient to disturb the regular course of actions, and to throw all into confusion. Nature is faithful in displaying to us things as they exist: our erroneous conceptions are the result of misguided education, or of wrong impressions made during childhood. The harsh treatment, for example, of a tender boy by a merciless pedagogue, may produce an intimate connection between study and distress,

* Elements of Criticism, chap. 1

stress, so as to give an aversion to books, never to be conquered. Inculcate into a boy that his fate depends on the motion of the planets: in spite of reason, he will be addicted to judicial astrology. There are men who, from some unlucky impression made on them when children, are as much afraid of a harmless cat as of a fierce lion.

One of Mr Locke's most beautiful chapters is upon association of ideas. He shows the bad effects that certain ideas unhappily connected or associated, have upon the understanding and upon the affections. " The ideas, he observes, of
" goblins and sprights, have really no
" more to do with darkness than with
" light; yet let but a foolish maid in-
" culcate these on the mind of a child,
" and raise them there together, possibly
" he shall never be able to separate them
" so long as he lives, but darkness shall

" ever after bring with it these frightful
" ideas, and they shall be so joined that
" he can no more bear the one than the
" other." He proceeds to inform us,
" That some such wrong and unnatural
" combinations of ideas will be found to
" establish the irreconcileable opposition
" between different sects of philosophy
" and religion. That which thus capti-
" vates reason, and leads men of since-
" rity blindfold from common sense,
" will, when examined, be found to be
" some independent ideas, of no alliance
" to one another, by education, custom,
" and the constant din of their party, so
" coupled in their mind that they always
" appear together, and can be no more
" separated than if they were but one
" idea, and they operate as if they were
" so. This gives sense to jargon, de-
" monstration to absurdities, and consist-
" ency to nonsense, and is the founda-
" tion

" tion of the greatest, I had almost said,
" of all the errors in the world."

Association of ideas is a plentiful source of speculation. Mr Locke has given a fine opening to the subject of ill founded associations, and it deserves well to be prosecuted. It ought to be a chief concern in the tutor to prevent in his pupil an association between truth and error. Truth is in great danger from such an association: error cannot for ever stand its ground against reason; and if it happen to be detected, the whole tumbles down together like the cemented parts of an old fabric. Thus it has fared with the Christian religion. The minds of men were more enslaved by the Church of Rome, than their bodies formerly by the republic of Rome. Reason was blasted in the bud; and people, through superstition and bigotry, were prepared to embrace every absurdity, as readily

readily as the most sacred truths. The Romish Church, taking advantage of this blindness, sedulously inculcated every doctrine that tended to aggrandize their Dalai Lama. Its humble disciples made no difficulty to swallow, even without a wry face, the rankest absurdities, direct contradictions not excepted, of which the *credo quia impossibile est*, is a notable instance. When, upon the revival of arts and sciences, the light of reason began to dawn, and men ventured to think for themselves, how came it that the Church of Rome was not apprehensive of its danger? It was so accustomed to absolute authority, as to have no dread of a rebellion; and after whole nations had thrown off its yoke, and proclaimed liberty of conscience, it was too late to think of a remedy. So far Christianity was a gainer. But unhappily, the absurd doctrines grafted on revelation, have led many well meaning persons to reject it it totally. Opinions aſſociated by education, and confirmed by cuſtom, are, as Mr Locke expreſſes it, ſo coupled in the mind, as not to be ſeparated more than if they were but one idea. Had the Chriſtian Revelation been preſerved in its original purity, promulgating immortality to the world, with a diſtribution of rewards and puniſhments in a future ſtate, I am confident that it would have been embraced by the wifeſt and the beſt men, and adhered to by all without heſitation, not even excepting ſuch as may entertain doubts or ſcruples about the ſtrength of the evidence.

To reject the Chriſtian Revelation, is a ſad effect of ill aſſociated opinions; and yet ſuch aſſociation may have a ſtill worſe effect: it may produce vicious practice, much leſs tolerable than erroneous principles. Many pious teachers aſſociate religion with a rigidity of manners;

too

too strict for any human being. What consequences are to be expected from such an association? Young persons, miserable under such unnatural restraint, seldom fail of becoming either hypocrites or open profligates. Our Saviour says, "My yoke is easy and my burden light." These teachers maintain his yoke to be galling and his burden heavy. Religion is given us for our good, and in obeying its precepts there is great satisfaction: such doctrines on the contrary render it harsh and uncomfortable. Zealous disciples of *Law upon Christian perfection* must be miserable in this life; and if they break loose from their fetters, they must be miserable in the life to come.

Opulence confessedly, with luxury and selfishness its concomitants, are the most obvious causes of the decay of patriotism in Britain; but they are not the only causes. An association of repugnant opinions

opinions has contributed to that woful effect. Above a century ago, paffive obedience and non-refiftence to the arbitrary will of a fingle perfon, was a ruling principle in politics: it was fubftituted to the love of our country, and was carried to as ridiculous an extreme as ever chivalry was. Reafon at laft prevailed, after much oppofition: the abfurdity of a whole nation being flaves to a weak mortal, remarkable perhaps for no valuable qualification, became apparent to all. It was not difficult to forefee the confequence: down fell the whole fabric, the found parts with the infirm. And men now laugh currently at the abfurd notions of their forefathers, without thinking either of being patriots, or of being good fubjects.

THE affociations above mentioned, are but a few of the many that tend to miflead people from a juft way of thinking.

Formerly,

Formerly, this nation was over-run with imaginary ghosts and apparitions; for simple people give a ready ear to wonders; and the more wonderful, the more firm is their belief. A child in the nursery listens greedily to a dreadful story. It believes and trembles; and, if not of a bold spirit, is domineered by the impression for life. I could name persons, whom even the most profound philosophy has not delivered from the fancied association of terror with darkness. What skill then does not the cultivation of the heart and head require, when after the ordinary discipline of school and college, men of all ranks are found to be infected with wrong biasses and irregular associations, which stand firm even against the most solid reasoning! Let this consideration actuate those who preside over the education of youth. How deep are the impressions, good or bad, that are made in childhood! As
this

this is the proper period for impreſſions, what have not teachers to anſwer for who neglect it. With reſpect to religion in particular, the moſt important branch of education, it is in the power of a ſenſible tutor to inſtil into his pupil, notions ſo juſt and clear as to ſecure him againſt every hurtful error. Above all, let it be inculcated, that religion is the great ſupport of morality, that it is our ſtrongeſt ſafeguard againſt the diſtreſſes of life, that it is conſiſtent with every rational enjoyment; and upon the whole, that its direct tendency is to make its votaries happy.

APPENDIX I.

Things to be got by Heart for improving the Memory.

BENEVOLENCE *recommended.*

A Mouse by accident coming under the paw of a lion, begged hard for life, urging that clemency is the fairest attribute of power. The lion generously set it at liberty. The mouse afterward observing the lion entangled in the toils of the hunter, flew to his assistance, gnawed the net to pieces, and set him free. Hence an useful lesson, Neglect no opportunity of doing good; for even the lowest may happen to be useful to the highest.

MODERATION *recommended.*

A boy, fond of a butterfly, pursued it from flower to flower. He thought to

surprise

surprise it among the leaves of a rose; then to cover it with his hat as it was feeding on a daisy: he followed it from blossom to blossom; but the nimble creature, still eluded his grasp. Observing it now half buried in the cup of a tulip, he rushed forward, and happened unluckily to crush it. The poor boy chagrined at his rashness, was addressed by the dying insect in the following words: " Behold " the fruit of thy impetuosity! Know " that pleasure is but a painted butterfly, " which may be indulged for amuse- " ment; but if embraced with too much " ardour will perish in thy grasp."

Honesty *rewarded.*

The Prince of Conti, highly pleased with the intrepid behaviour of a grenadier at the siege of Philipsburgh 1734, threw his purse to him, excusing the smalness of the sum. Next morning the grenadier came to the Prince, with a couple

couple of diamond rings and other jewels of value. "Sir," said he, "the gold I found in your purse, I presume was intended for me; but the jewels I bring back to your highness, having no claim to them. You have, soldier," answered the pince, "your honesty entitles you to them as much as your bravery entitles you to the gold."

Honesty rewarded.

The Cardinal Farnese, stiled the Patron of the Poor, gave public audience once a week to indigent persons in his neighbourhood, and distributed money among them according to their wants. A poor woman presented herself one day with her daughter, a beautiful creature of about fifteen years of age. "My Lord," says she, "I owe for the rent of my house five crowns; and my landlord threatens to turn me to the street, unless I pay the sum within a week. What I beg of "you

"your eminence is, to interpose your sa-
"cred authority, and protect us from the
"violence of that cruel man, till by our
"industry we procure the money for
"him." The cardinal after writing a
billet, "Go," says he, "to my steward
"with this paper, and receive from him
"five crowns." The steward upon sight
of the billet told out fifty crowns. The
poor woman refused to take above five,
saying "she expected no more, and that
"surely it was a mistake." They agreed
to refer the matter to the cardinal himself. "It is true," said he, "there is a
"mistake: give me the paper and I will
"rectify it." He gave the rectified billet to the woman, saying, "such can-
"dour and honesty deserve a recom-
"pense. Here I have ordered you five
"hundred crowns. What you can spare
"of it, lay up as a dowry for your
"daughter in marriage."

DISHONESTY *punished.*

AN usurer, having lost an hundred pounds in a bag, promised a reward of ten pounds to the person who should restore it. A man having brought it to him, demanded the reward. The usurer, loth to give the reward now that he had got the bag, alleged after the bag was opened, that there were an hundred and ten pounds in it when he lost it. The usurer being called before the judge, unwarily acknowledged, that the seal was broken open in his presence, and that there were no more at that time but a hundred pounds in the bag. " You say," says the judge, " that the bag you lost
" had a hundred and ten pounds in it."
" Yes, my Lord." " Then," replied the judge, " this cannot be your bag, as it con-
" tained but a hundred pounds. There-
" fore, the plaintiff must keep it till the
" true owner appears: and you must
" look

" look for your bag where you can find
" it."

CHARITY *recommended.*

ZACCHOR and Efreff begged Morat their tutor, to permit them to visit the curiosities of Aleppo. He gave them a few aspers to expend as they thought proper; and on their return, he enquired how they had bestowed the money, " I," said Zacchor, " bought some of the finest " dates Syria ever produced: the taste " was exquisite." " And I," said Efreff, " met a poor woman with an infant at " her breast: her cries pierced me. I " gave her my aspers; and grieved that " I had not more." The dates, said Morat to Zacchor, will in a few hours be converted into mere excrement; but Efreff's charity will be a lasting blessing, and contribute to his happiness, not only in this life, but in that to come.

FRIENDSHIP.

Antonius after the battle of Philippi, being in close pursuit of Brutus, Lucullus, to preserve the life of his friend Brutus, surrendered himself to the soldiers, pretending to be Brutus. Being brought before Antonius, he said, "My friend "Brutus is not taken prisoner, and I "hope the gods will not suffer it. As I "have imposed upon your soldiers, I am "ready to suffer what severity you please "to inflict upon me." Antonius turned to the soldiers and said, "Don't be "discouraged fellow soldiers: you have "brought me a better prize than what "you fought for." He then embraced Lucullus, applauded his friendship, wished to have him for a friend, and found him such for ever after.

FRIENDSHIP.

The good Damon being condemned by Dionysius tyrant of Syracuse to suffer a capital punishment, he requested permission to set his affairs in order, which lay at a distance from the capital. Permission was granted upon his finding one to answer for his return, and to suffer death in his stead if he failed. This the tyrant did as a show of humanity, not imagining that such a man would be found. Pythias offered to answer for his friend, and Damon was set at liberty. When the day of execution drew near, the tyrant had the curiosity to visit Pythias in his dungeon. He rallied him for his folly in presuming that Damon would return to suffer death, and be as foolish as Pythias himself had been. My Lord, said Pythias with a firm voice, I would suffer a thousand deaths, rather than that my friend Damon should fail in any article of his honour. He cannot fail: I am as confident of his virtue as of my own existence. But I beseech the gods, to preserve the life of my Damon.

Oppose him ye winds! and suffer him not to arrive till by my death I have redeemed a life, of more value a thousand times than my own; of infinite value to his lovely wife, to his innocent children, to his friends, to his country. Dionysius was confounded, and awed by the dignity of these sentiments, so opposite to his own. He hesitated, looked down, and retired without speaking. The fatal day arrived, Pythias was brought forth, and walked to the place of execution, with a serious but satisfied air. Dionysius was already there, sitting pensive and attentive to the behaviour of the prisoner. Pythias on the scaffold addressed the assembly with a chearful countenance, "My prayers are heard," he cried, "the "gods are propitious! You know, my "friends, that the winds have been con- "trary. Damon could not come, he "could not conquer impossibilities. He "is on his way, hurrying on, accusing
"himself

" himself and the adverse winds. But I haste to prevent him. Executioner, Do your duty." As he pronounced these words, a distant voice was heard; and, stop, stop the execution, was proclaimed by the crowd. A man came at full speed. In an instant he was off his horse, on the scaffold, and held Pythias straitly embraced. "You are safe," he cried, "you are safe my friend, my beloved; the gods be praised, you are safe!" Pale with anguish in the arms of his Damon, Pythias replied in broken accents, fatal haste, cruel impatience! What envious powers have wrought impossibilities to destroy you? But I shall not be wholly disappointed; since I cannot save you, I will die with you. Dionysius heard, and beheld all with astonishment. His heart was touched, his eyes were opened; and he was sensible for the first time of the force of virtue and of friendship. Descending from his throne,

throne, he afcended the fcaffold. Live, live, ye incomparable pair, he exclaimed. You have taught me the reality of virtue and of friendfhip. Live happy, live renouned, and, oh, form me by your precepts, as you have invited me by your example, to be worthy of being your friend.

LIBERALITY.

CROESUS reproaching Cyrus the Great, for fquandering the public treafure among his favourites, Cyrus, in order to juftify his liberality, defpatched circular letters to his grandees, defiring from each of them, for a preffing occafion, as much money as they could fpare. As it amounted to a much greater fum than Cyrus had beftowed on them, he faid to Crœfus, " I am not lefs in love with " riches than other princes, but am a " better hufband of them. See what my " fmall donations have procured me;
" not

"not only many friends, but more faith-
"ful treasurers than those can be who
"serve for hire."

VERACITY.

The Duke d'Ossuna having leave from his Catholic Majesty to release some galley slaves, such as he should think the best deserving of pardon, went on board the Admiral Galley at Barcelona, and asked several of the slaves what were the crimes that had sent them to the galleys. Every one endeavoured to excuse himself, that it was out of malice, that the judges were corrupted, or such like. The same question being asked at a little sturdy fellow, he acknowledged that he was justly condemned; for being in want of money, that he had robbed a man on the high-way. On which the Duke gave him a blow over the shoulders with a cane, saying, "You rogue, why should
"you be among so many honest inno-
"cent

" cent men? Get you out of their com-
" pany, for fhame."

The moſt pleaſing Sort of REVENGE.

IN a war between the French and Spaniards in Flanders, a foldier, being ill treated by a general officer, and ſtruck feveral times with a cane, ſaid coolly, that the officer ſhould ſoon repent of it. A ſhort time after, the ſame officer commiſſioned the colonel of the trenches to find him out a bold fellow, who for a reward would undertake a dangerous piece of work. The foldier mentioned offered his ſervice; and taking with him thirty of his comrades, performed the work with ſucceſs. The officer highly commended him, and gave him a hundred piſtoles, the reward promiſed. The foldier, after diſtributing them among his comrades, turned to the officer and ſaid, " I am, Sir, the foldier you abuſed
" fifteen days ago, and I told you that
                                " you

"you would repent it." The officer melted into tears, threw his arms around the foldier's neck, begged his pardon, and inftantly gave him a commiffion.

Fruits *of* Industry.

A GENTLEMAN of the county of Surry, having an eftate in land of L. 200 yearly, kept the whole in his own hand. Finding that this did not anfwer, he was forced to fell the half to pay his debts, and he fet the remainder to a tenant for one and twenty years. Toward the end of the leafe, the tenant afked the landlord if he would part with his land. " Prithee tell " me," fays the landlord, " how it fhould " come that I could not live upon twice " as much being my own, and yet that " you, having but the one half and pay- " ing rent for it, have been able in twen- " ty years to buy it? " Sir," faid the farmer, " when any thing was to be " done, you faid, Go and do it; but I
" always

" always faid, Let us go and do it; and
" fo not only faw my bufinefs done, but
" affifted."

CONJUGAL AFFECTION.

THE Emperor Conrad, having in the fiege of Wiltfburgh reduced the inhabitants to great extremity, and having taken pity of the women who were innocent, permitted them to depart from the town with what luggage they could bear on their backs. The Duchefs took Guelpho her hufband on her back; and all the other women following her example, iffued forth, laden not with gold and filver, but with men and children. The Emperor pleafed with this ftratagem, took the Duke into favour with all his adherents.

CONJUGAL AFFECTION.

SHE meets a fon of age in the woods. Bending, he weeps over a gray ftone. " Here,"

"Here," he said, "sleeps the spouse of my love; here, I reared over her the green turf.—Many were our days on the heath. We have turned away our feet from young trees, left we might crush them; and we have seen them again decay with years. We have seen streams changing their course; and nettles growing where feasted kings. All this while our joy remained; our days were glad. The winter with all its snow was warm, and the night with all its clouds was bright. The face of Minalla was a light that never knew a wane; an undecaying beam around my steps. But now she shines in other lands; When, my love, shall I be with thee?"

PRIDE.

A YOUNG lady of rank and fortune went out to walk in her father's woods. "Pray madam," said the gray-headed steward.

steward, "may I humbly intreat that "you will not go far from home: you "may meet with strangers who are ig- "norant of your quality." "Give your "advice" answered she, "when desired. "I admit of no instructions from ser- "vants." She walked on with satisfac- tion, enjoying a clear sky, and a cool breeze. Fatigue seized her, regardless of high birth; and she sat down on a smooth spot at the side of a high road, expecting some equipage to pass, the owner of which would be proud to convey her home. After long waiting, the first thing she saw was an empty chaise, conducted by one who had formerly served her fa- ther as a postilion. "You are far from "home Madam, will you give me leave "to set you down at my old master's."— "Prithee fellow, be not officious." Night was fast approaching, when she was ac- costed by a country man on horseback. "Mistress, will you get on behind me, "Dobbin

"Dobbin is sure-footed, you shall be set down where you will, if not far off, or much out of my way." "*Mistress!*" exclaimed she, "how dare you presume." —No offence, said the young man, and rode away, humming the song *I love Sue*.

It was night: the clouds gathered, the leaves of the trees rustled; and the young woman was terrified with what she took for strange sounds. There came an old man driving an empty dung cart. "Friend," said she with a humble accent, "will you let me go with you?"

Pride is the most galling burden a person can walk under. Prudence saves from many a misfortune: pride is the cause of many.

Against idle Disputes.

One of our ancient British Princes set up a statue to the Goddess of Victory

where

where four roads met. In her right hand was a spear; and the left rested on a shield, one face of which was gold, the other silver. It happened one day, that two knights completely armed, the one in black, the other in white, came up to this statue from opposite parts. This golden shield, says the black knight—golden shield, interrupted the white knight, if I have eyes, it is silver. I know nothing of your eyes, replied the black knight; but I know that the shield is gold. The dispute ended in a challenge. After fixing their spears, they flew with impetuosity at each other; and both of them fell to the ground much bruised. A Druid who came by, showed them their mistake; and gave them this lesson, "Never to enter into a dispute till "you have fairly considered both sides "of the question."

Ludicrous.

Sir William Lilly, a famous painter in the reign of Charles I. agreed beforehand for the price of a picture he was to draw for a rich London alderman, who was not indebted to nature either for shape or face. The picture being finished, the alderman endeavoured to beat down the price, alleging that if he did not purchase it, it would ly on the painter's hand. "That's your mistake," says Sir William, "for I can sell it at double "the price I demand." "How can that "be," says the alderman, "for 'tis like "no body but myself?" "True," replied Sir William; "but I will draw a tail to "it, and then it will be an excellent "monkey." Mr Alderman, to prevent being exposed, paid down the money demanded, and carried off the picture.

Smort

Smart Repartee.

One evening at Button's coffee-house, Mr Pope, who was remarkably *crooked*, and a set of literati, poring over a manuscript of the Greek poet Aristophanes, found a passage they could not understand. A young officer, who stood by the fire, begged that he might be permitted to look at the passage. "Oh!" says Mr Pope sarcastically, "by all means, " pray satisfy the young gentleman's cu- " riosity." The officer, considering a while, said that there only wanted a note of interrogation to make the passage intelligible. Piqued at being outdone by a redcoat, "Pray" says Pope, "what is " a note of interrogation? A note of in- " terrogation," replied the youth, "is " a little crooked thing that asks ques- " tions."

The Cunning outwitted.

A GENTLEMAN, attacked in his chariot by a highwayman, furrendered his purfe containing about forty guineas; adding that robbery was an infamous calling, and that the highwayman would do better to put what he had done upon a reputable footing, by exchanging his blunderbufs with the purfe. " With all my " heart," fays the highwayman; and delivered his blunderbufs. The gentleman, turning it againft him, threatned to fhoot if he did not inftantly reftore the purfe. " You may do as you pleafe," replied the highwayman; " but I muft " ufe the freedom to tell you, that the " biter is bit, for the blunderbufs is not " loaded."

Temperance and Content.

BEN HADI the Dervis entertained his Sovereign Harum the Calif of Egypt with the following account of his life. Caled my father, full of years and of benevolence to his fellow creatures, waited with entire resignation for the hour that Providence had appointed to be his last. Finding death fast approaching, he called me to his bed-side. "My son," said he, "my beloved and only son, I have "no wealth to bequeath you; but I will "leave you two of the greatest secrets of "nature, namely, one to acquire wealth "to the utmost bounds of your wishes; "and one to pass a long and chearful "life, free of distress either of mind or "body. But in order to benefit by these "secrets, there are certain things which "you must solemnly promise to per-"form." I did so, resolving from the bottom of my heart to be obsequious to my father's commands. "Take," said he, "this book written by Bedreddin, "famous for sanctity of life. Peruse it "over and over with the deepest atten-"tion; it will envigorate the seeds of

"virtue sowed by me in your tender
"mind, so as to guard you against the
"contagion of vice; without which you
"never can be worthy of that inestimable
"treasure. When you are thoroughly
"conscious of meriting that reward,
"break the seals of this letter (putting
"it into my hand): in it the whole my-
"stery is contained. But should you
"open it before you are proof against
"every temptation, the characters will
"instantly vanish, and leave you in the
"dark as much as before." Embracing
me with the utmost tenderness, he ex-
pired in my arms. When time had mo-
derated my grief, I thought of my lega-
cy. I passed whole days in imagined
scenes of power and grandeur, in exalt-
ing my favourites and depressing my
enemies. I was resolved that my palace
should be sumptuous above any that the
greatest monarch possesses, that the very
pavement of it should be solid gold. But

as the awful promise I had made was essential, I opened the precious book. I found the diction sweet and elegant, and the sentiments refined. But above all, its precepts of morality and religion charmed me. I read it over and over, meditated upon it night and day; and squared my conduct by these precepts, till I became habitually as well as naturally virtuous. At last, I perceived a total change in my disposition. I roved no longer upon grandeur; nor held riches in any esteem. I had indeed secured uninterrupted health by temperance; but I had no wish to prolong my life beyond the days allotted by Providence. The whole of my study was to be steady in virtue, and to guard against every temptation. In a word, I became indifferent about the secrets contained in the letter. I opened it however in obedience to my father's will, and read what follows. " If thou hast read with
" profit

" profit the volume bequeathed, and mo-
" delled thy conduct according to its
" dictates, already doſt thou poſſeſs the
" promiſed bleſſings. Temperance is
" the only ſecret to baniſh diſeaſe, and
" to prolong a chearful life. And con-
" tent will reliſh the ſimple things that
" temperance requires; whereas un-
" bounded riches are an invincible temp-
" tation to abandon real good in the
" purſuit of imaginary pleaſure."

At my father's death, I was within the years of eighteen, ignorant of the world and of its corruptions. A young man without experience, is liable to various temptations, partly from imitation, and partly from his irregular appetites; and without a truſty monitor ſeldom fails to be led aſtray. My beloved father, to whom I am indebted for every bleſſing of life, contrived this ſtratagem,

like

like a trusty monitor, to secure me against every temptation.

You behold here, continued the Dervis to his Sovereign, the utmost limits of my wishes. My cell, which you have deigned to visit, is neat, though far from costly. I want for none of the conveniencies of life; nor do I covet any of its superfluities. Dainties serve only to deprave the appetite, and to render more wholesome food insipid. Riches and splendor are air bubbles, which lose their imagined value when they become familiar. My dread Sovereign, when you attain to my age, you will regard ambition and other empty phantoms that fill the mind during the heat of youth, to be vain delusions. To you virtue will then appear in her native charms. When sick of such vanities, virtue, which, like the laurel flourishing in perpetual bloom,

suffers

suffers no decay, shall prove your sweetest consolation.

> The Dervis ended, and in Harum's ear
> So charming left his voice, that he awhile
> Thought him still speaking, still stood fix'd to hear.

As stratagems like the foregoing, to guard virtue during youth, are seldom happy in the invention, and as little in the execution, good education, prosecuted with unremitting care, is the only stratagem that can be relied on by parents for securing good conduct in their children. Benevolence, it is certain, and all the other moral virtues, may be impressed on the tender mind, so successfully as to become a second nature.

LUDICROUS.

A CHESHIRE-MAN set sail for Spain,
To deal in merchandize;
No sooner he arriv'd there, than
A Spaniard he espies,
  Who said, " You English dog, look here,
" What fruits and spices fine
" Our land produces twice a-year,
" You've no such fruit in thine."
THE Cheshire-man ran to his hold,
And brought a Cheshire-cheese,
Then said, " You Spanish dog behold!
" You've no such fruits as these.
  " Your land produces twice a-year,
" Rich fruit and spice you say;
" But such as now my hands do bear,
" Our land gives twice a-day."

CHEARFULNESS *recommended*.

THE honest heart, whose thoughts are clear
From fraud, disguise, and guile,
Need neither fortune's frowning fear,
Nor court the harlot's smile.

The greatness that would make us grave,
Is but an empty thing;
What more than mirth would mortals have?
The chearful man's a king.

In Praise of Content.

No glory I covet, no riches I want,
Ambition is nothing to me,
The one thing I beg of kind heaven to grant,
Is a mind independent and free.

With passions unruffled, untainted with pride,
By reason my life let me square:
The wants of my nature are cheaply supply'd,
And the rest are but folly and care.

The blessings, which Providence freely has lent,
I'll justly and gratefully prize;
While sweet meditation and chearful content
Shall make me both healthy and wise.

How vainly, thro' infinite trouble and strife,
Do many their labours employ;
Since all that is truly delightful in life,
Is what all, if they will, may enjoy.

COMPASSION.

Pity the sorrows of a poor old man,
Whose trembling limbs have borne him to your door,
Whose days are dwindled to the shortest span,
Oh! give relief, and heaven will bless your store.
Those tatter'd cloaths my poverty bespeak,
Those hoary locks proclaim my lengthen'd years;
And many a furrow in my grief-worn cheek
Has been the channel to a flood of tears.
Yon house erected on the rising ground,
With tempting aspect drew me from my road;
For plenty there a residence has found,
And grandeur a magnificent abode.
Hard is the fate of the infirm and poor!
Here as I crav'd a morsel of their bread,
A pamper'd menial drove me from the door
To seek a shelter in an humbler shed.
Oh! take me to your hospitable dome;
Keen blows the wind, and piercing is the cold!
Short is my passage to the friendly tomb,
For I am poor and miserably old.
Should I reveal the sources of my grief,
If soft humanity e'er touch'd your breast,

Your hands would not with-hold the kind relief,
And tears of pity would not be repreſt.
Heav'n ſends misfortunes; why ſhould we repine;
'Tis Heaven has brought me to the ſtate you ſee;
And your condition may be ſoon like mine,
The child of ſorrow and of miſery.
A little farm was my paternal lot,
Then like the lark I ſprightly hail'd the morn;
But ah! oppreſſion forc'd me from my cot,
My cattle dy'd and blighted was my corn.
My daughter, once the comfort of my age,
Lur'd by a villain from her native home,
Is caſt abandon'd on the world's wide ſtage,
And doom'd in ſcanty poverty to roam.
My tender wife, ſweet ſmoother of my care,
Struck with ſad anguiſh at the ſtern decree,
Fell, ling'ring fell, a victim to deſpair,
And left the world to wretchedneſs and me.
Pity the ſorrows of a poor old man,
Whoſe trembling limbs have borne him to your door,
Whoſe days are dwindled to the ſhorteſt ſpan,
Oh! give relief and heaven will bleſs your ſtore.

HAPPINESS *of the* MARRIED STATE.

AT Upton on the hill,
There live a happy pair;
The swain his name is WILL,
And MOLLY is the fair;
Ten years are gone and more,
Since HYMEN join'd these two;
Their hearts were one, before
The sacred rites they knew.

SINCE which auspicious day,
Sweet harmony does reign;
Both love, and both obey:
Hear this, each nymph and swain,
If haply care invade,
As who is free from care?
Th' impression's lighter made
By taking each a share.

PLEAS'D with a calm retreat,
They've no ambitious view;
In plenty live, not state,
Nor envy those that do.
Sure pomp is empty noise,
And cares encrease with wealth;
They aim at truer joys,
Tranquillity and health.

With safety and with ease
Their present life doth flow;
They fear no raging seas,
Nor rocks that lurk below:
May still a steady gale
Their little bark attend,
And gently fill each sail,
'Till life itself shall end.

Happiness of the Married State.

Old Darby, with Joan by his side,
I have often regarded with wonder,
He's dropsical, she is dim-ey'd,
Yet they're ever uneasy asunder:
Together they totter about,
Or sit in the sun at the door;
And at night, when old Darby's pipe's out,
His Joan will not smoke a whiff more.

No beauty nor wit they possess,
Their several failings to cover:
Then what are the charms, can you guess,
That make them so fond of each other?
'Tis the pleasing remembrance of youth,
The endearments that youth did bestow,

The thoughts of paſt pleaſure and truth,
The beſt of our bleſſings below.

Those traces for ever will laſt,
Nor ſickneſs nor time can remove:
For when youth and beauty are paſt
And age brings the winter of love,
A friendſhip inſenſibly grows,
By reviews of ſuch raptures as theſe;
The current of fondneſs ſtill flows,
Which decrepit old age cannot freeze.

Virtue *praiſed*.

Would you the bloom of youth ſhould laſt?
'Tis virtue that muſt bind it faſt;
An eaſy carriage, wholly free
From ſour reſerve, or levity;
Good natur'd mirth, an open heart,
And looks unſkill'd in any art;
Humility, enough to own
The frailties, which a friend makes known,
And decent pride, enough to know
The worth, that virtue can beſtow.

These are the charms, which ne'er decay,
Tho' youth and beauty fade away,

And time, which all things else removes,
Still heightens virtue and improves.

Vanity of Praying for EARTHLY BLESSINGS.

THE man to Jove his suit preferr'd;
He begg'd a wife. His prayer was heard.
A wife he takes. And now for heirs
Again he worries heav'n with prayers.
Jove nods assent. Two hopeful boys
And a fine girl reward his joys.

ONCE more, he cries, accept my prayer;
Make my lov'd progeny thy care.
Let my first hope, my fav'rite boy,
All fortune's richest gifts enjoy.
My next with strong ambition fire:
May favour teach him to aspire;
'Till he the step of pow'r ascend,
And courtiers to their idol bend.
With ev'ry grace, with ev'ry charm,
My daughter's perfect features arm.
If Heav'n approve, a father's bless'd.
Jove smiles, and grants his full request.

The first, a miser at the heart,
Studious of ev'ry griping art,
Heaps hoards on hoards with anxious pain;
And all his life devotes to gain.
He feels no joy, his cares increase,
He neither wakes nor sleeps in peace;
In fancy'd want (a wretch complete)
He starves, and yet he dares not eat.

The next to sudden honours grew:
The thriving art of courts he knew:
He reach'd the height of power and place;
Then fell, the victim of disgrace.

Beauty with early bloom supplies
His daughter's cheek, and points her eyes.
The vain coquette each suit disdains,
And glories in her lover's pains.
With age she fades, each lover flies,
Contemn'd, forlorn, she pines and dies.

When Jove the father's grief survey'd,
And heard him heaven and fate upbraid,
Thus spoke the god. By outward show,
Men judge of happiness and woe:
Seek virtue; and, of that possest,
To providence resign the rest.

Superiority of VIRTUE above VICE.

VIRTUE and Vice, two mighty powers,
Who rule this motley world of ours,
Difputed once which govern'd beft,
And whofe dependents moft were bleft;
And both the doubtful point confent
To clear by fair experiment.
For this fome mortal they declare,
By turns fhall both their bounties fhare.

ON Hodge they fix, a country boor,
As yet rough, ign'rant, carelefs, poor:
Vice firft exerts her pow'r to blefs,
And gives him riches to excefs:
With gold fhe taught him to fupply
Each rifing wifh of luxury:
Hodge grew at length polite and great,
And liv'd like Minifter of State:
He fwore with grace, got nobly drunk,
And kept in pomp his twentieth punk.

ONE morning, as in eafy chair,
Hodge fate with ruminating air,
Vice, like a lady fair and gay,
Approach'd, and thus was heard to fay,
" Know, favoured mortal, know that I
" The pleafures of thy life fupply;

"I rais'd thee from the clay-built cell,
"Where want, contempt, and flav'ry dwell;
"And (as each joy on earth is fold)
"To purchase all, I gave thee gold.
"My name is Vice!"—Cried Hodge, and leer'd,
"Long be your mighty name rever'd!
"Forbid it, Heav'n! thus bleſs'd by you,
"That I ſhould rob you of your due;
"To wealth, 'twas you that made me heir,
"And gave, for which I thank you, care;
"Wealth brought me wine, 'tis paſt a doubt,
"And wine—ſee here's a leg! the gout:
"To wealth my French ragout I owe,
"Whence ſcurvy, pains, and aſthmas flow."
Enrag'd and griev'd, away ſhe flew,
And with her gifts from Hodge withdrew.

Now in this ſad repentant hour,
Celeſtial Virtue try'd her pow'r;
For wealth content the goddeſs gave,
Th' unenvy'd treaſure of the ſlave!
From wild deſires ſhe ſet him free,
And fill'd his breaſt with charity!
No more loud trumpets riot breeds,
And temp'rance gluttony ſucceeds.

B b b HODGE,

Hodge, in his native cot at rest,
Now Virtue found, and thus addrefs'd:
" Say, for 'tis yours by proof to know,
" Can Virtue give the blefs below?
" Content my gift, and temp'rance mine,
" And charity, tho' meek, divine!"
With blufhing cheeks, and kindling eyes,
The man tranfported thus replies:
" My goddefs! on this favour'd head,
" The life of life, thy bleffings fhed!
" My annual thoufands when I told
" Infatiate ftill I figh'd for gold;
" You gave content, a boundlefs ftore,
" And rich indeed! I figh'd no more—
" With temp'rance came, delightful gueft!
" Health, tafteful food, and balmy reft;
" With charity's feraphic flame,
" Each gen'rous focial pleafure came;
" Pleafures which in poffeffion rife,
" And retrofpective thoughts fupplies!
" Long to atteft it may I live,
" That, all Vice promifes, you give."

Caveat

Caveat against being smit with an out-side.

A tender Miss, whom mother's care
Bred up in wholesome country air,
Far from the follies of the town,
Alike untaught to smile or frown;
Her ear unus'd to flatt'ry's praise,
Unknown in woman's wicked ways;
Her tongue from modish tattle free,
Undip'd in scandal and bohea;
Nor cards she dealt, nor flirted fan,
A stranger to quadrille and man;
But simple liv'd, just as you know
Miss Chloe did—some weeks ago.

As now the pretty innocent
Walk'd forth to taste the early scent,
She tripp'd about the murm'ring stream,
That oft had lull'd her thoughtless dream.
The morning sweet, the air serene,
A thousand flow'rs adorn'd the scene;
The birds rejoicing round appear
To chuse their consorts for the year;
Her heart was light, and full of play,
And, like herself, all nature gay.

On such a day, as poets sing,
A Butterfly was on the wing;

From bank to bank, from bloom to bloom,
He stretch'd the gold-bespangled plume:
Now skims along, and now alights
As smell allures, or bloom invites;
Now the violet's freshness sips;
Now kiss'd the rose's scarlet lips;
Becomes anon the daisy's guest;
Then press'd the lily's snowy breast;
Nor long to one vouchsafes a stay,
But just salutes and flies away.

 The virgin saw with rapture fir'd;
She saw, and what she saw desir'd.
The shining wings, the starry eyes,
And burns to seize the living prize:
Her beating breast and glowing face
Betray her native love of dress.
Ensnar'd by empty outward show,
She swift pursues the insect-beau;
O'er gay parterres she runs in haste,
Nor heeds the garden's flow'ry waste.
The nymph o'er every border flew,
And kept the shining game in view:
As hov'ring o'er the tulip's pride
He hung with wing diversify'd,

Caught in the hollow of her hand,
She held the captive at command.
  Flutt'ring in vain to be releas'd,
He thus the gentle girl addrefs'd:
" Loofe, gen'rous virgin, loofe my chain;
" From me what glory can'ft thou gain?
" A vain, unquiet, glitt'ring thing,
" My only boaft a gorgeous wing;
" From flow'r to flow'r I idly ftray,
" The trifler of a fummer's day:
" Then let me not in vain implore,
" But leave me free again to foar."
  His words the little charmer mov'd,
She the poor trembler's fuit approv'd.
His gaudy wings he then extends,
And flutters on her finger ends:
From thence he fpoke, as you fhall hear,
In ftrains well worth a woman's ear.
  " When now thy young and tender age
" Is pure and needlefs to engage;
" Unknowing all, to all unknown,
" Thou liv'ft, or prais'd, or blam'd by none.
" But when, unfolding by degrees
" The woman's fond defire to pleafe,

                                                 " Thou

"Thou fett'ft thy little charms to fhow,
"And fports familiar with the beau;
"Thou in the midnight-ball fhalt fee
"Things apparel'd juft like me.
"If charm'd with the embroider'd pride,
"The victim of a gay outfide,
"From place to place, as me juft now,
"The glitt'ring gewgaw you purfue,
"What mighty prize fhall crown thy pains?
"A Butterfly is all thy gains!"

VIRTUE *praifed*.

Now fpring begins her fmiling round,
Lavifh to paint th' enamell'd ground;
The birds exalt their chearful voice,
And gay on every bough rejoice.
The lovely graces hand in hand,
Knit in love's eternal band,
With dancing ftep at early dawn,
Tread lightly o'er the dewy lawn.
Where-e'er the youthful fifters move,
They fire the foul to genial love.
Now by the river's painted fide,
The fwain delights his country-bride:

While,

While, pleas'd, she hears his artless vows;
Above the feather'd songster wooes.
Soon will the ripen'd summer yield
Her various gifts to ev'ry field;
Soon fruitful trees, a beauteous show,
With ruby-tinctur'd births shall glow;
Sweet smells, from beds of lilies born,
Perfume the breezes of the morn.
The sunny day, the dewy night,
To rural play my fair invite;
Soft on a bank of violets laid,
Cool she enjoys the ev'ning-shade;
The sweets of summer feast her eye:
Yet soon, soon will the summer fly.

ATTEND, my lovely maid, and know
To profit by the moral show;
Now young and blooming thou art seen,
Fresh on the stalk, for ever green;
Now does the unfolded bud disclose
Full-blown to sight the blushing rose:
Yet, once the sunny season past
Think not the coz'ning scene will last;
Let not the flatt'rer hope persuade:
Ah! must I say that this will fade?

For see the summer posts away,
Sad emblem of our own decay.
Now winter, from the frozen north,
Drives his iron chariot forth;
His grisly hand in icy chains
Fair Tweda's silver flood constrains:
Cast up thy eyes, how bleak and bare
He wanders on the tops of Yare!
Behold his footsteps dire are seen
Confess'd on many a with'ring green.
Griev'd at the sight, when thou shalt see,
A snowy wreath clothe ev'ry tree,
Frequenting now the stream no more,
Thou fly'st, displeas'd, the barren shore.
When thou shalt miss the flow'rs that grew
But late to charm thy ravish'd view,
Shall I, ah horrid! wilt thou say,
Be like to this another day?

Yet, when in snow and dreary frost
The pleasure of the field is lost,
To blazing hearths at home we run,
And fires supply the distant sun;
In gay delights our hours employ,
We do not lose, but change our joy;

Happy

Happy abandon every care,
To lead the dance, to court the fair,
To turn the page of ancient bards,
To drain the bowl and deal the cards.
But when the beauteous white and red
From the pale afhy cheek is fled;
When wrinkles dire, and age fevere,
Make beauty fly we know not where;
The fair whom fates unkind difarm,
Have they for ever ceas'd to charm?
Or is there left fome pleafing art,
To keep fecure a captive heart?

UNHAPPY love! might lovers fay,
Beauty, thy food, does fwift decay;
When once that fhort-liv'd ftock is fpent,
What art thy famine can prevent?
Virtues collect with early care,
That love may live on wifdom's fare;
Tho' extacy with beauty flies,
Efteem is born when beauty dies.
Happy to whom the fates decree
The gift of heav'n in giving thee:
Thy beauty fhall his youth engage;
Thy virtues fhall delight his age.

Though the chief purpose of this collection is to improve the memory by exercise, it is not however the only purpose. Nothing is admitted but what tends to mend the heart. I have beside in view, to initiate young persons in the art of pronunciation; and accordingly the things I have selected are in various stiles.

APPENDIX II.

Excerpts *from a young Gentleman's Common-place-book, being the History of his first Excursion after completing his College-Education. September* 1734.

IN my journey through Fife I met with nothing remarkable, save a good country in the state of nature. The bishopric of Durham is reckoned one of the finest districts in England. Fife, like it, spreads every where into little green hills and valleys; but no planting, no inclosing, poor crops of corn except upon the coast, and very little grass. The spirit of improvement is indeed beginning in that country; and planting and inclosing will give it a very fine appearance. Cupar, the county town, is pleasantly situated on the banks of the Eden. A bleaching-field is lately made there, which will promote the linen manufacture in that country, hitherto little advanced. In our road from this town to Dundee, a curious group of figures struck us, that would be a good subject for a picture. A little woman was shearing corn on a little ridge. Behind her was a boy about eight or nine, gleaning what fell from her hand. At the side of the corn stood a cradle with an infant in it, rocked by a girl younger than the boy. At some distance a little cow was tethered, and by it a little dog lying. I missed nothing of the family but the little cat, which I suppose was left at home to guard the little house. How few are the necessities of nature, and how easily provided for? May we not imagine this little woman as contented, as the great Lord of the manor?

Dundee is a trading town, advantageously situated on the river Tay, two miles above

above where it falls into the sea. The river is there two miles broad and makes a fine appearance. The town has been encreasing ever since the Union in the number of inhabitants and goodness of the houses. They are now at work about a town-house, the plan of which they have from Mr Adams. Though Dundee is the largest town in Angus, yet Forfar is the county town. It stands in the great valley of Strathmore, that runs from Perth north-east to the sea almost in a straight line, about fifty miles long, and betwixt four and five broad; bordered on either side by hills rising gently on the south side, and on the north by the famous Grampians a little more elevated. 'Tis a beautiful strath or valley adorned with houses and planting, and intersected with rivers descending from the hills. Forfar is a royal burgh, poor indeed, having little to brag of but its antiquity. King Malcolm Canmore held his first parliament

ment there, and the ruins of his palace are yet to be seen. The town is situated at the side of a lake, within which there is an island where Queen Margaret retired after her husband Malcolm Canmore's decease. There is a tradition in the town of Forfar, that to this queen, canonized afterward for a saint, we owe the custom of the grace-drink: she established a rule, that whoever staid till grace was said, was to be rewarded with a bumper. This piece of history diverted us and occasioned some reflections. In the *first* place, it appears surprising that one should be eternized for such a trifle. I know not but this may have been the principal flourish in the preamble of Queen Margaret's patent for saintship. But when we examine the nature and course of things, the surprise vanishes. Our nation was then in its infancy, examples of courage, public spirit, devotion, learning, &c. rare. Every thing makes a figure in a country not overstocked with examples of the same kind. In the next age, it required the building a church or mortifying an estate to gain the character of saint, purchased by our Margaret at so much easier a rate. In the first ages, men were esteemed heroes for subduing a robber or for killing a wild boar. Hercules reigns to this day for no higher exploits; and in this country, it is reported that the origin of Lord Sommerville's family is owing to the destroying an overgrown worm, the figure of which animal, and of the chieftain in the act of killing, remain cut in stone in the old kirk of Linton. Turn over the lives of the ancient Greek philosophers, and many of them will be found eternized for a saying or opinion, for which a man would not think one jot the better of his parish minister. Happy are they who delight in fame, to live in such ages! The same circumstances of a people may also explain how the grace-cup,

cup, a thing that among us at prefent would be but the maggot of a day, fhould have grown into a general cuftom. Scotland being then in its infancy, deftitute of laws, deftitute of cuftoms, rude even in the art of fpeech, manners and cuftoms would be eafily introduced to fill a vacuity; and when a cuftom is once introduced, even upon the flighteft foundation, it continues long in vigour, becaufe there is nothing to put it out of its place. A nation advanced to maturity is in a different condition. Every thing there being reduced to form and figure, there is little room left for new cuftoms or new manners. Here however a diftinction occurs between cuftoms that gain ftrength by habit, and thofe that are naturally fluctuating, fuch as the fafhions of drefs. But at prefent being not much inclined to deep fpeculation, I yield to nature in her purfuit of more airy game. And here I obferve, that whatever may be be thought of the world turning worse and worse, the men in those ancient times have not been more religious than they are now. Were people bribed to go to church by a good dinner after sermon, we should find churches as much crowded as ever. In former ages too, it seems we were satisfied with the form of religion as well as at present. But what comes of the ladies all this while; for sure Queen Margaret was too polite to think of a bumper as a reward to them. Whatever might be done in private, they would not be inclined to exert their prowess in public. In drinking-bouts and love-intrigues, they strictly follow the scripture, not to let their left know what their right is doing. A lady to whom I was talking of this defect in Queen Margaret's plan, gave me a ready answer. Fix the men, says she, and no fear of the ladies. This solution must be acknowledged ingenious as well as ingenuous: whether solid or no, the ladies can best tell. For my part, I would incline to put it upon a better footing: the women in all ages have been remarkable for their piety; and therefore I suppose that this law was made for the men only: the ladies will observe decency at least, without a bribe.

Were I to describe Forfar in the heroic strain, I should say that the inhabitants are a very hospitable people. Entertained we were by the chief magistrate, whose doors fly open to all strangers. It is expected indeed that you leave vails answerable to your entertainment. If this ceremony happen to be neglected, officers of the household are in the way, who modestly take you by the sleeve, and, out of zeal for your reputation, put you in mind of your duty.

The finest thing seen here, is an edifice of the most perfect model, appearing to be as sweet a dwelling as one would wish for. It has been exposed to sale for years; and yet, which is strange, no purchaser has been found. 'Tis true, it is not richly furnished, and riches go a great way in those days. For my part, I willingly would have taken a lease of it, but had not money for the purchase. This building was not made with hands, though of human architecture. It passes by the name of Miss Lyon.

From Forfar our company came by invitation to Gallery, the seat of Mr Fullerton, a gentleman who made his fortune in the West Indies, and now for some years has been settled in his native land, where he passes his time with ease and chearfulness, free from the hurry of business and fracas of great towns, which he says he is heartily tired of. He is indeed an agreeable old man, has a very good house with fine gardens situated

upon

upon the river of Montrose in Strathmore. He diverted us with an incident that happened lately. He has relations in the county of Cornwall. One of them, a young Esquire, made him a visit this summer, of three or four weeks. The tender mamma, who had dismal notions of Scotland, begged her child for God's sake to return home before the weather should break, which might be dangerous in so wild a country. Prepossessed with this opinion, the young gentleman with his governor arrived at Gallery. Could they fail to be surprised with the fineness of the gardens, variety of the fruits, and gaiety of the fields? Above all, some orange and almond-trees struck the sage governor with admiration. An orange-tree in a pot had by some accident been left in the kitchen-garden: the grass had grown up that nothing was seen but the plant. The curious governor, whom you may suppose a member of the Royal Society,

ciety, espied this wonder first, and called upon his pupil to behold. Mr Fullerton, with a well acted indifference, seemed to know nothing of the matter, only that to be sure it had been some seed of the orange-tree, blown there by the wind, or accidentally dropt by the gardener. The man was ravished at the discovery— the pocket-book was pulled out, day and place marked, with all circumstances. This possibly may be heard of in the transactions of the Royal Society. Thus travellers first impose upon themselves, and then upon the world.

ABERDEEN at present is one of the most flourishing towns in the kingdom. They tell me, that since the memory of man the inhabitants are doubled. Their own manufactures are exported annually to the value of near a hundred thousand pounds Sterling, which is mostly returned in specie. The inhabitants of the
shire

shire are an induſtrious people, man, wife and child employed; abundance of good company in the town itſelf, a more hoſpitable people are no where to be met with.

Episcopacy with the liturgy of the Church of England, prevails much more here than in the ſouthern parts; and in proportion, gentlemen who are no friends to the preſent eſtabliſhment. However, of late many of them have got over the ſcruple of taking oaths, in order to ſerve their friends at elections: for there is no reaſon to believe that there is any change in their political principles. To one unacquainted with the world and its manners, this muſt appear extremely ſhocking. To call upon God to witneſs a lie; to promiſe, to bind myſelf in the moſt poſitive terms, when I never intend to perform; what, it will be ſaid, can be more wicked? And yet, when I look abroad into the world.

world, and find so many gentlemen of honour acting this part with scarce any remorse, I am puzzled and cannot help stopping short to consider, whether after all this practice is so criminal. If it be, it is surely the single instance in nature of a great crime attended with scarce any remorse or indignation. But this cannot be. All crimes must give us abhorrence; and be we ever so well read in Grotius and Puffendorf, there is no rule given us to judge of human actions so certain as what we draw from our own heart. The merit or demerit of actions is in proportion to the good or hurt they do. Lying, swearing falsely, breach of promise, are criminal as tending to the dissolution of society, which cannot subsist without mutual faith and trust among men. This is what makes treachery so odious a crime. On the other hand, whatever words a man uses, yet if it be clearly understood, that no faith is intended to be given

given or received, they are of no moment. Thus it is with the common civilities and compliments paſsing among men, which one would be reckoned a fool to depend on. Thus, to go a little deeper, cuſtom-houſe oaths now-a-days go for nothing. Not that the world grows more wicked, but becauſe no perſon lays any ſtreſs upon them. The duty on French wine is the ſame in Scotland as in England. But as we cannot afford to pay this high duty, the permiſsion underhand to pay Spaniſh duty for French wine, is found more beneficial to the revenue, than the rigour of the law. The oath however muſt be taken that the wine we import is Spaniſh, to entitle us to the eaſe of the Spaniſh duty. Such oaths at firſt were highly criminal, becauſe directly a fraud againſt the public; but now that the oath is only exacted for form's ſake, without any faith intended to be given or received, it becomes very little different from

from saying in the way of civility, " I am, Sir, your friend, or your obedient servant." And in fact, we every day see merchants dealing in such oaths whom no man scruples to rely upon in the most material affairs. I could wish, that the taking oaths to the government, when the heart goes not along, were but as innocent. So far is plain, that when a man takes oaths in order to get into power, is trusted, and betrays his trust, nothing can be more vitious. But let us suppose he takes the oaths to preserve his estate, to give bread to his family, or to serve his friend at an election who is friendly to the government; how far is this criminal? We must examine first, how far it was right in the Parliament to impose such oaths. This matter ought to be handled tenderly; yet there is no avoiding entering into it. Here the distinction naturally calls up betwixt a manifest rebellion, and a civil war occasioned by a controverted title. Of the last sort, none will question the Revolution to have been; and those gentlemen who did, and do stand out against the Revolution, must be allowed to be acting against private interest upon a principle of conscience. One would think it hard to treat such gentlemen as common robbers or rebels. All laws, human and divine, teach us to treat them with lenity. And indeed in the main, they are so treated. Yet of some severities, they have reason to complain. For example, if they be allowed the protection of the government, for what good reason should they not be permitted to gain a livelihood in any private way they are capable of? Why may not a man be an advocate, though it does not go clearly with his mind, that the Chevalier is a bastard? This surely is a hardship; and the people I am talking of, will be apt to hold the oath of abjuration, to be rigorous and unjust. If they

bow

bow the head in the house of Rimmon, they have the Assyrian for their example, and the prophet for their authority. To be peaceable subjects without attempting to disturb the Government, they think is all that can reasonably be exacted of them. It must be confessed, there is less to be said in justification of those who swallow the oaths, for no better reason than to assist their friend at an election. Yet even here, it may be thought, that such oath, cannot be very criminal where no harm is done or intended, it being the same to the Government whether the one or the other candidate, both of them friends, be returned. This is a theme I thought well worthy of consideration. It lessens our horror to find that our countrymen are not so criminal as we at first imagine. If there be any weight in this apology, it ought to teach all governments to be tender in imposing oaths: if rigorous or unreasonable, they will scarce

answer

answer the end; and their multiplicity tends to break faith and confidence among men. Balancing however ill with good, it may be a question, whether we have been great sufferers by the political oaths imposed since the Revolution. On the one hand, there is the evil tendency we have been speaking of: on the other, these oaths have been useful in making men better subjects, No honest man, by whatever motive prevailed on to take the oaths, but must consider them as some pledge of his obedience; and it is fact, that many a one has thus been carried imperceptibly from his old friends, and become at last a hearty friend to the present establishment*.

---

* The danger of multiplying oaths is well urged by this young gentleman, and yet, the benevolence of youth has prompted him to extenuate them. "But "it is dangerous to withdraw the smallest peg in the "moral edifice, for the whole will totter and tumble. "Men creep on to vice by degrees. Perjury, in or- "der to support a friend, has become customary of
late.

THE following adventure happened lately in Aberdeenshire. Though the little god of Love has become a domestic animal, yet his wings are not so much shortened, but that goose-like, he can now and then make a short flight. Gordonio, the ordinary fate of younger brothers, was left to shift for himself with a very small patrimony. By great penury and much industry, he has scraped together about ten thousand pounds. When about fifty he fell in love; the first time that any passion had touched his breast, save that of gain. Where had it lurked all this while? The young lady was averse,

" late years; witness fictitious qualifications in the
" electors of parliament-men, which are made effec-
" tual by perjury : yet such is the degeneracy of the
" present times, that no man is the worse thought of
" on that account. We must not flatter ourselves
" that the poison will reach no further. A man who
" boggles not at perjury to serve a friend, will in
" time become such an adept as to commit perjury
" to ruin a friend when he becomes an enemy."
Sketches, vol. IV. p. 175.

verse, the man at once became a new creature. The change was first observed in his dress and air. The rolled stockings disappeared, his breeches had buckles at the knees; and what was a new sight in Aberdeen, were held up by a large buckle behind. Fine linen, powdered wigs, followed of course: the man now walks erect with an open countenance. In a word, he would not be known to be the sloven that walked about in a pace slow and circumspect, his eyes upon the ground, fear and care imprinted on his visage. The fort at last surrendered, and it is computed the siege cost him above five hundred pounds. What cannot gold perform? He has been married above a twelvemonth, and is now the most hospitable man in Aberdeen. Every body approves of his taste, his wife being a chearful and agreeable woman. He is sparing of nothing but of his words, and to such a degree, that he still retains an old

old bye-word, "All in good time;" which indeed he has right to appropriate, the phrase being expressive of his own fortune. I do not remember a story that comes nearer to that of Cymon and Iphigenia; only this is within the bounds of nature. Cymon is represented a stupid fool; and yet to fall in love at first sight, requires no slight degree of sensibility. But to let that pass, our Cymon is a strong instance how uncertain our guesses are about the characters of men. Fifty years of his life had passed, when, by accident, he became acquainted with the lass that made the first impression on his heart. Had not this happened, he would have jogged on in the old way, and no mortal have known, nay not he himself, what sort of a man he is. Had Oliver Cromwell been much addicted to music, agriculture, or any trifling amusement, it might have kept him at home without thinking of overturning the

the conſtitution. Upon ſuch ſlender hinges do the greateſt events turn.

The county of Murray, is one of the fineſt in the kingdom; in its ſituation and climate, very much reſembling Eaſt Lothian. Elgin the county-town is beautifully ſeated in a plain upon the river Loſſy, which runs into the ſea about four miles below. Its courſe lies betwixt two lakes; that of Spenzie on the weſt, which covers a great quantity of land; that of Coats on the eaſt, of a much leſs ſize. The old caſtle of Duffus, the ſeat of the family, is ſituated in a plain, cloſe to the lake of Spenzie, formerly a mile from it. This change was wrought by ſeveral late inundations of the river Loſſy, which filling the lake with ſand, raiſed the water and made it overſpread much ground. I believe it might be poſſible to drain this lake altogether; but belonging to many proprietors, it is not eaſy to make

make them join in a common meafure. One thing they would lofe. A great quantity of fwans come down from the hills and refort there in winter. Murray is a fandy foil, efpecially toward the fea. There is a great track of land eaſt of the river Findhorn, which in the year 1690, was overblown with fand, and to this day, has a difmal appearance, occafioned by a pernicious cuftom of pulling bent upon the fand-hills at the fhore, now prohibited by Act of Parliament. In the road from Innes to Gordonfton on the eaſt fide of the river Loffy, for a mile together, you meet with bare gravel like what is at the mouth of great rivers : but every now and then, there are pillars of fand about feven feet high, with grafs atop. This formerly was all a fandy foil about feven feet deep above the gravel. The country people by paring the furface for covering their houfes, laid the fand open to the wind, which in a few years overfpread overspread a great space of land. But luckily the wind blowing strongly from the south-west before the sand was covered with grass, the whole was driven into the sea; and now one will scarce discern where it has been. Sir Robert Gordon's estate lies a few miles west from the river Lossy upon the sea. Such another accident some years ago overspread a part of this estate with sand, particularly a piece of link ground. The sand rotted the surface of the links, and the south wind not only blew the new sand into the sea, but with it the sand that had formed the links; and to the surprise of every body, the ground below was fine soil, and had actually carried corn, for it was lying in ridges.

The mosses in this county and in Aberdeenshire, furnish the only fuel they have at home; for there is no coal but what is brought by sea, nor is there any wood

wood in the county, at least in the low parts of it. These mosses are formed by the rotting of wood; and there is scarce a moss that has not much wood, not quite dissolved. Nothing is more evident: and yet it puzzles me; for by this account the whole surface of the earth must have been moss. Berwickshire lies low, and many parts of it wet. It was once all wood, which surely was not all cut down for use. How comes it then, that there is not the least vestige of moss in the lower part of a county where it was most natural to expect it?

The house of Innes is one of the most commodious old houses in this country. The ground storey is vaulted. The principal apartment above the vaults, consists of two grand rooms, one of them forty-eight feet long; the two storeys above contain ten well proportioned bed-chambers, and the house is provided with a handsome

handsome scale stair-case. Over the great door there is the following inscription, *Nulli certa domus*, No man's habitation is certain. Does this inscription show a spirit of resignation; or can vanity be discerned lurking under the mask of humility? Compare this with the inscription on the standard of the great Saladin. THIS BLACK SHIRT IS ALL THAT SALADIN CONQUEROR OF THE EAST SHALL CARRY TO HIS GRAVE. Sure there was no vanity here, but an angelic moderation preserved amid illustrious victories. It was a great atchievement of a private gentleman to build the house of Innes, near two hundred years ago; and what he had reason to value himself upon. To see such an inscription over the little door of a cottage, would indeed be ludicrous; no less so than what is reported of a little man elected Provost of Aberdeen, who, amid the congratulations of his acquaintance, laid his hand upon his breast,

and

and declared that after all he was but a mortal man. Possibly one of an exalted soul would class the builder of Innes with the Provost of Aberdeen. For my part, I should value myself much upon so handsome a performance; and am therefore of opinion, the inscription is less allied to vanity than to resignation. In matters of opinion, there is no fixed standard to judge by. Our opinions are various like our temper, because it has great influence on them.

INVERNESS, 10th October. In this country a new scene opens which those of the south know little of. The people here are generally divided into tribes or clans, who acknowledge a chief, whom they more willingly obey than their king. No safety for a man who would live independent: he is obliged to inlist himself into one or other clan. A gentleman, in order to affront a neighbour, stole away

the

the dead body of a near relation, whom the neighbour was preparing to bury. The friends were convened for the burial; but behold the corpſe was gone. This occaſioned a Juſticiary trial. The only witneſſes were the criminal's accomplices, all of them of his own name. They depoſed point blank that none of them had ſo much as heard of the thing, till ſpread all over the country. No body doubted of the perjury. I was ſtunned, and could not help obſerving to one of the Judges, that the ſouls of theſe people were as much at their chieftain's devotion, as their bodies. In a converſation about clanſhip, a gentleman of the name of Grant, a Lieutenant in an independent company, blundered out his true ſentiments, that he would rather hear of the Grants ſtealing three cows, than hearing of one ſtolen from them. This is ſavage, but not ſo much as may be imagined. The clans hate one another, but are remarkably honeſt

nest to those of their own name. And their mutual depredations are rather to be considered as reprisals than as theft. The case here is precisely the same as between Scotland and England, before and for some time after the Union of the two Crowns. To enliven the conversation, I took the part of my blunt friend, and flourished the best I could upon this topic. The Captain was ravished. I said further, that the old Romans were all divided into clans. When I found I was listened to, my vanity led me to display a little of my learning. I observed that in the Roman state, their tribes had like our clans a common name; that when a tribe grew numerous, it was divided into what the Romans called *families;* and in some of the most populous tribes, the families were again divided into *stripes* or branches. In the last case, every man had four names: the first was his proper name, such as *Caius* or *Lucius*, or Peter or John among us. The second

second was the name of the tribe, the third, of the family, the fourth, of the branch. I added, that clanship is a great bulwark against absolute monarchy and tyrannical government, it being easier to subdue one man than ten thousand firmly united by all the ties of blood and friendship. For that reason, the Roman Emperors never were at rest, till they broke and dissolved all the clan-connections. They began with opening the succession of land to females; and proceeded step by step, till there remained no traces of clanship more than now in England, or in the southern counties of Scotland.

REFLECTING afterwards on this conversation, several things occurred to me. Succession with us has an air of accident more than of design. We admit female-succession; and yet none of my mother's relations can succeed to me. If we follow nature, why should brothers or sisters be excluded though related only by the mother? If our views be political, why not exclude women altogether and keep estates within the name?

In this country we see no good effects of clanship; constant quarrels and somewhat like natural antipathy between clans; and of course entire neglect of the public. We find nothing similar in the Roman story, if the struggles be excepted betwixt the Patricians and Plebeians, which, on the part of the latter, were for liberty not superiority. How to be accounted for, that the private tribe-combination did not in the least impair their patriotism? As the mind of man is of a limited capacity, the more regard we have for one set of men, the less is left to bestow upon others; consequently the affection a Roman had to bestow upon one of another tribe could not be great: every one knows how little regard the Patricians and Plebeians had for one another. As clanship therefore muſt be unfavourable to patriotiſm, we cannot ſufficiently admire the Roman method of education, which ſupported that noble affection againſt the undermining influence of the clan-connection. But now what ſhall we ſay of our family feuds, of which ſcarce a footſtep among the Romans. This ſeems a puzzling queſtion. The Roman clanſhip was an union or ſociety among equals: our clanſhip, a petty government of ſubjects united under one head or chieftain. Here light breaks in. A ſociety among equals tends to defence more than offence: a ſociety of ſubjects under a common chief, tends to offence as much as to defence.

Was the Roman clanſhip a proper conſtitution in a great ſtate? On the one hand, where one is born a ſubject of a ſtate ſo extenſive as ſcarce to make any connection

tion among individuals, he has nothing but merit and engaging manners to depend on. The acting a part in the middle of an unconcerned multitude, is next to acting in a solitude. On the other hand, every individual of a clan has the support of the whole; and is besides emboldened, by acting in the sight of many who are concerned in him as friends and relations, who he knows will take his part right or wrong. This resolves all into birth, with little or no regard to personal merit, which is attended with every inconvenience that is remarkable in hereditary nobility.

N. B. THE reader will judge, whether this young gentleman had not only made good use of his time, but had also been in the practice of a common-place-book, long before this first excursion.

F I N I S.

www.ingramcontent.com/pod-product-compliance
Lightning Source LLC
Chambersburg PA
CBHW051736300426
44115CB00007B/591